The Search for Origins

in the

Twentieth-Century

Long Poem

The Search for Origins in the Twentieth-Century Long Poem: Sumerian, Homeric, Anglo-Saxon

Joe Moffett

MORGANTOWN 2007

West Virginia University Press, Morgantown 26506
© 2007 by West Virginia University Press
All rights reserved.
First edition published 2007 by West Virginia University Press
Printed in the United States of America

13 12 11 10 09 08 07 06   9 8 7 6 5 4 3 2 1

ISBN 978-1-933202-12-9 (paperback)

Library of Congress Cataloguing-in-Publication Data
The Search for Origins in the Twentieth-Century Long Poem: Sumerian, Homeric, and Anglo-Saxon/ Joe Moffett.
viii, 180 p.   22 cm.

1. American poetry–20th century–History and criticism. 2. Postmodernism (Literature)–United States. 3. Literary form–History–20th century. 4. Reading. I. Title. II. Moffett, Joe.

IN PROCESS
Library of Congress Control Number: 2007924807

Printed in USA by BookMobile.
Cover design by Than Saffel. Page design by Katie Denton/Than Saffel

Material Reprinted by Permission:
Chapter 3, "Master, I Was the Freshest of All Your Readers": Postcolonialism and Postmodern Self-Reflexivity in Derek Walcott's *Omeros*; Copyright 2005 from "'Master I Was the Freshest of All Your Readers': Derek Walcott's *Omeros* and Homer as Literary Origin" by Joe Moffett. Reproduced by permission of Taylor & Francis Group, LLC., http://www.taylorandfrancis.com

West Virginia University Press has no responsibility for the persistence or accuracy of URLs for third-party websites referred to in this publication, and does not guarantee that any content on such websites is, or will remain, accurate or appropriate.

Contents

1   "Returning to the Origin and Bringing Something Back" in the Twentieth-Century Long Poem

33 Charles Olson's *The Maximus Poems* and Armand Schwerner's *The Tablets*: From Late Modernist to Postmodernist Long Poem

61 "Master, I Was the Freshest of All Your Readers": Postcolonialism and Postmodern Self-Reflexivity in Derek Walcott's *Omeros*

91 Narrating the Origins of the Nation: Geoffrey Hill's *Mercian Hymns* and "An Apology for the Revival of Christian Architecture in England"

123 "A New Myth of Origin": Judy Grahn's *A Chronicle of Queens* and Popular Culture

154 Conclusion: Origins and the Modern/Postmodern Divide

161 Bibliography

172 Index

Preface

In *The Dream Songs*, John Berryman jokes that

> The only happy people in the world
> are those who do not have   to write long poems:
> muck, administration, toil.

In these lines, Berryman hints at the idea that underlies much of twentieth-century Anglo-American poetry: that the long poem is the premier poetic endeavor, one that necessarily occupies years, sometimes decades, of the author's life. The hard work—the toil—that poets put into their long poems is reflected by the effort readers must put into understanding these challenging works. A number of excellent scholarly studies already exist that detail the formal elements of the long poem. In *The Search for Origins in the Twentieth-Century Long Poem*, I adopt a different approach and instead identify one of the salient themes that persists in a number of otherwise dissimilar poems. The more one looks for it, the more one sees that poets of the last century are fascinated with the past in their long poems, and in attempting to connect (or reconnect as it may be) with that perceived past, they engage in what I call a "search for origins." In my introductory chapter, I detail precisely what I mean with this phrase and explore some of the implications of poets' forays into the past. Suffice it to say now, however, that this search leads poets in many different directions, and part of my objective here is to chart a few of those divergent paths.

Preface

Along this journey, I have been aided by a number of people whom it gives me great pleasure to thank. Over the last several years I have worked on this project, I have been aided often by Brian McHale's keen insights. I want to acknowledge those who read various drafts and versions of this project or offered suggestions along the way: Kathleen McNerney, Lisa Weihman, Dennis Allen, Mary Ann Samyn, Gerry LaFemina, and Sandy Baldwin, as well as the blind reviewers for the West Virginia University Press whose suggestions at the late phase of this project helped me see it with fresh eyes and, I hope, improve it in many ways. Patrick W. Conner at the Press has been more than I could have ever hoped for in an editor and friend. Joey Connelly, Andrew Gates, and Matthew Clarke offered editorial help at the end of this project. Despite the efforts of these wonderful people, any errors that persist are my own responsibility.

My third chapter appeared in print under the title "'Master I was the Freshest of All Your Readers': Derek Walcott's *Omeros* and Homer as Literary Origin" in a slightly different form in the January–March 2005 edition of *LIT: Literature Interpretation Theory*. My thanks go to Taylor and Francis for allowing me to reprint it here. Chapter 4 was delivered under the title "Questioning the Origins of the Nation: Anglo-Saxonism and Geoffrey Hill's *Mercian Hymns* and 'An Apology for the Revival of Christian Architecture in England'" at the 34th Annual Twentieth-Century Literature and Culture Conference, hosted by the University of Louisville on February 23–25, 2006. My thanks go to the organizers of that event for inviting me to share my ideas and to those in attendance for listening.

Thanks go to my father and mother, Joe and Darla Moffett, as well as my sister, Cheyenne, for all their encouragement. Neil Ritter and Sally Ritter offered support in many ways. I want to dedicate my work on this book to my wife Kelly and son Devon. Without their support, none of it would have been possible.

1

"Returning to the Origin and Bringing Something Back" in the Twentieth-Century Long Poem

The Long Poem and the Search for Origins

I want to begin with my thesis: a number of long-poem writers in twentieth-century literature are preoccupied with a search for origins. But the nature of the search changes. For modernist poets, the search usually entails divining or recovering lost originary moments;[1] for postmodernists, it typically means questioning, revising, or even repudiating origins identified by modernists. To make my discussion more concrete, later in this chapter I will focus on three specific originary moments that are engaged by poets in the twentieth century. First I need to work backward and address a couple of fundamental questions: Why origins? Why the long poem?

To be sure, the long poem, the form alternatively labeled by Octavio Paz as the "extensive poem," is used variously by poets of the last century.[2] Texts such as Hart Crane's *The Bridge* (1930) or Galway Kinnell's *The Book of Nightmares* (1971) pick up where Whitman left off by assessing the place of poetry in a democratic

Chapter One

culture.³ Other works examine the psychological pressure on the individual in contemporary society, such as the so-called confessional poetics of John Berryman in *The Dream Songs* (1969). Poems such as *Meadowlands* (1996) by Louise Glück and *The Queen of Wands* (1982) by Judy Grahn explore issues of gender. The long poem proves a vital force in poetry engaged in language play and polysemy, from Louis Zukofsky's *"A"* (1978) to Charles Bernstein's "The Lives of the Toll Takers" (1994) and Susan Howe's *The Europe of Trusts* (1990).⁴ This list only hints at the wide array of subject matter and approaches evident in the long poem in the last century.

Although the long poem is heterogeneous in character, a search for origins is one theme that binds together a number of otherwise quite disparate texts.⁵ The *Oxford English Dictionary*'s second definition of the term "origin" is the one most applicable to my purpose: "That from which anything arises, springs or is derived; source of being or existence; starting-point." When I say long poems "search for origins," I mean that they attempt to use origin or "starting-point" cultures as a way to examine their own present cultures and social conditions. A partial list of long poems engaged in this pursuit would include H. D.'s *Helen in Egypt* (1961), Basil Bunting's *Briggflatts* (1966), Geoffrey Hill's *Mercian Hymns* (1971), and Derek Walcott's *Omeros* (1990). I will look at these texts, as well as a number of others, later in this chapter.

Some poets declare their search for origins directly. Seamus Heaney remarks in his short poem "Kinship,"

> I step through origins
> like a dog turning
>
> its memories of wilderness
> on the kitchen mat.⁶

The term "origin" often conjures up images of a primal state, one from which the present moment is presumed to descend. The search for origins entails a fundamental inquiry into the past. It

"Returning to the Origin and Bringing Something Back"

asks questions like, where did we come from? Is the present really a progression from the past? Is there a way for us to fully comprehend that which came before us? It also asks, preeminently, can we connect with the past in some tangible way? This last question is of utmost importance to modernist poets, as I will show shortly.

More often, poets do not use the term, and we must look to the subtext of their work for evidence of origin-seeking. Whether explicit or not, the search for origins is a ubiquitous endeavor, cutting across a number of writers and literary movements over the course of the last century. Certainly not every writer of the long poem is concerned with origins, but I hope to show by the breadth of my examples here the degree to which this is a widespread phenomenon.

So if seeking origins allows poets to understand the present by looking into the past, then the question remains: why is the long poem the genre chosen for this line of inquiry? The long poem is well suited to this enterprise because it lacks strict genre conventions that govern other literary forms: a long poem does not need to follow a reasoned line of thinking as a critical essay does; there is no need for plot and character development as in a novel; the long poem eclipses the lyric poem in its size and capaciousness. In the fragmentary poems that make up modernism, process is valued over product, and this too makes the long poem an important tool as poets use it as a meditative device. Margaret Dickie points out that the long poem is synonymous with American modernism. She writes, "[W]hat is American Modernism? It is the long writing of the long poem."[7] Dickie believes the form is "long in the time of composition, in the initial intention, and in the final form"; she concludes, "[T]he Modernist long poem is concerned first and last with its own length."[8] By virtue of its very size, the modern long poem offers poets ample space with which they can think about origins.

In terms of literary history, long poems preoccupied with origins might be seen as inheritors of the origin-seeking evident in the epic-inspired poems of the past.[9] Perhaps the primary difference between the ambitious texts of the twentieth century and those that came before them, however, is the influence of new archaeological discoveries in the latter half of the nineteenth and beginning of the twentieth centuries.[10] These advances transformed poets' perceptions of the past by exhuming originary sites and cultures.[11] However, poems do not need to state a preoccupation with archaeological findings to be informed by originary thinking.

Indeed, Ezra Pound's early long poem (or sequence, depending on how one reads it) "Hugh Selwyn Mauberley" (1920) can be taken as a representative example of the kind of originary thinking I have been discussing. Pound is not deeply invested in archaeology. His poem might be best remembered for the way it illustrates the devastating effects of World War I on the modern psyche. The speaker in "Mauberley" famously declares,

> The age demanded an image
> Of its accelerated grimace,
> Something for a modern stage,
> Not, at any rate, an Attic grace.[12]

Pound contrasts his current cultural moment with the grandeur of the "Attic grace." The "grimace" of the modern age pales in comparison with the glories of the classical age. A return to the attitudes or approaches to living characteristic of that earlier era would presumably remedy the problems of the present; there could be a movement away from the "disillusions as never told in the old days,/hysterias, trench confessions,/laughter out of dead bellies" of contemporary existence.[13] Thus, for figures like Pound, a return to an origin is a corrective gesture, an attempt to rectify the shortcomings of the age.

Pound's poem exhibits a desire to connect with the past that runs throughout modernism. John B. Vickery speaks of the "elegiac" mood of modernism, one which calls attention to that which has been lost over time.[14] Writers like Pound are engaged in identifying and reevaluating historical moments from which current social practices either originated or deviated—they are seeking

"Returning to the Origin and Bringing Something Back"

origins in other words. Usually writers adopt worldviews or attempt to appropriate elements of culture (such as "Attic grace") which they perceive as belonging to earlier periods. The crucial term here is "perceive." Put simply, in this study I am less concerned with critiquing whether or not these poets are accurately depicting past cultures than I am in adequately representing their responses to their perceptions. If Pound is convinced he lives in a "botched civilization," an "old bitch gone in the teeth," his poetry must be viewed as an attempt to engage the past to offer solutions for present-day problems.[15] However right or wrong he appears in his assumptions from our historical perspective is a separate matter.

Let us look at an example of the way originary thinking is handled differently between a modernist and a postmodernist poet.[16] T. S. Eliot's account of what he labels the "auditory imagination" contains one of modernism's most memorable statements on the importance of origins:

> What I call the "auditory imagination" is the feeling for syllable and rhythm, penetrating far below the conscious levels of thought and feeling, invigorating every word; sinking to the most primitive and forgotten, *returning to the origin and bringing something back*, seeking the beginning and the end. It works through meanings, certainly, or not without meanings in the ordinary sense, and fuses the old and obliterated and the trite, the current, and the new and surprising, the most ancient and the most civilised mentality.[17]

Identifying the "origin" is central to Eliot's conception of the poet's task here. The poet must journey back into the past to recover the "old and obliterated" and "fuse" it with the "new and surprising." A longing to "return to the origin and bring something back" marks Eliot's own *Waste Land* (1922), which juxtaposes the past and present in a series of fragmentary images, drawn from Biblical, Arthurian, and other traditions, all assembled to identify the problems of post-World War I life. Paul de Man writes that the "quest for the experience of origination is lived with all the intensity of a truly spiritual aspiration" and a sense of that "spiritual aspiration" pervades Eliot's desire to tap into the origin in his long poem and in his statement on the auditory imagination.[18] Like Pound, Eliot finds origins offer him a chance to revivify the present, to identify the current ills of society.

Eliot's focus on the "primitive and forgotten" foregrounds the primitivist strain that runs throughout modernist conceptions of art and society.[19] In the same set of lectures from which the quote above derives, Eliot argues,

> Poetry begins . . . with a savage beating a drum in a jungle, and it . . . retains that essential of percussion and rhythm; hyperbolically one might . . . say that the poet is *older* than other human beings.[20]

Marianna Torgovnick's work on primitivism helps us to understand Eliot's thinking. She remarks that "*primitive* always implied 'original,' 'pure,' 'simple'" and later in her book adds "[t]he West seems to need the primitive as a precondition and a supplement to its sense of self: it always creates heightened versions of the primitive as nightmare or pleasant dream."[21] Like Edward W. Said's argument for Western views of "the Orient,"[22] Torgovnick examines the way westerners project identities onto peoples of other parts of the world. This is certainly the case in Eliot's description of the "savage." Torgovnick links concern with the primitive to a preoccupation with "beginnings" that I have called a search for origins: "Our interest in the primitive meshes thoroughly, in ways we have only begun to understand, with our passion for clearly marked and definable beginnings and endings that will make what comes between them coherent narrations."[23] If Eliot is producing a "narrative" about poetry, then it is one which must account for the "savage" in the "jungle," one which must go back to the origin to retrieve that which has been left behind—some missing "essential," to use his term.

"Returning to the Origin and Bringing Something Back"

Among postmodernists, Jerome Rothenberg has consistently entertained notions of origins. His engagement with originary thinking persists into the groundbreaking anthology he edited with Pierre Joris, *Poems for the Millennium*, published in 1995. This work offers an overview of modernism in its various forms. The first book of this two-volume set ends with a section entitled "A Book of Origins."[24] Rothenberg and Joris write about this section,

> It is impossible ... to present the work of such a radical or innovative modernism without mapping at the same time some features of the old worlds, brought newly into the present & viewed there as if for the first time, to help to show us where we are. In this way the *new* seeks the *old*, as in many ways the *old* has often sought the *new*.[25]

This passage comments on the modernist search for origins and specifically recalls Eliot's statement on the auditory imagination with its vocabulary of the "new" and the "old." Additionally, Pound's conviction that "[a]ll ages are contemporaneous in the mind" serves as one of the epigraphs for this part of *Poems for the Millennium*. Pound's statement encapsulates for Rothenberg and Joris the way origins are handled in modernism: as a source or historically distant moment which is brought into the present by virtue of the mind's ability to hold disparate historical moments simultaneously. Originary thinking operates in this way in some of the poems I examine in this book. Many texts attempt to tap into more than one originary moment at a time. David Jones's *The Anathemata* (1952), for instance, mixes Welsh and Anglo-Saxon sources.[26] For Jones, as much as Pound, "[a]ll ages are contemporaneous in the mind."

Rothenberg has spent a career editing one anthology after another, each examining alternative poetic traditions. These alternative traditions typically comprise poetry belonging to what Eliot called the "savage." For Rothenberg, however, "Primitive Means Complex," as he explains in *Technicians of the Sacred* (1968), a text which includes poems from Africa, Asia, and Oceania.[27] Rothenberg thus problematizes the Eliotic model of "a savage [poet] beating a drum in a jungle." Rothenberg is careful to point out the culture-specific nature of views of what is "primitive": "Measure everything by the Titan rocket & the transistor radio, & the world is full of primitive peoples," he writes, "But once change the unit of value to the poem or the dance-event or the dream (all clearly artifactual situations) & it becomes apparent what all those people have been doing all those years with all that time on their hands."[28] *Technicians of the Sacred* begins with a section entitled "Origins and Namings" and includes a selection of creation stories from a diversity of traditions.[29] These texts attest to the recurring human commitment to establishing origins and poetry's function as the reservoir for this kind of thinking. Rothenberg's project continues in many ensuing volumes, including *Shaking the Pumpkin* (1972), which focuses on Native American poetry.

Given the shrinking influence of poetry in twentieth-century public life,[30] it is little wonder why modernist poets like Eliot and Pound would turn to past cultures in which they believed poetic writing thrived and seemed to form a more integral part of the fabric of social discourse. With his complication of the concept of "primitive," Rothenberg illustrates the way postmodernist writers have taken up the modernist inquiry into origins as he alters the perspective one finds in Eliot. Thus, although a preoccupation with origins is common among both modernist and postmodernist poets, these two groups look at the issue from different points of view. Generally, modernists like Eliot wish to return to the past to modify and improve the present;[31] postmodernists seek to revise or even repudiate modernist searches for origins. In my case-study chapters to follow, I will look at specific postmodern long poems and seek to analyze some of the issues they raise as the poets go about evaluating the originary pursuits of modernism—themes like revisionism, postcolonialism, nation, and gender appear as a result.

I should stress, however, that while the search for origins has often been repudiated by postmodern poets, it is nevertheless present. This has implications for our understanding of postmodern literature by pointing to both continuity and discontinuity between modernist and postmodernist texts. I will consider the implications that recognizing similarity and difference among modernism and postmodernism has for our understanding of the last century's poetics in my concluding chapter.

To flesh out further what I mean by long poems that seek origins, I want to distinguish the influence of three historical periods—what I have been calling "originary moments"—on the twentieth-century long poem. I will address each of these periods by first, in this chapter, surveying texts that engage them, and then in the case-study chapters to follow I will examine the periods further by looking at their representation in specific postmodern texts. I choose here to look at the periods most often identified as "Sumerian," "Homeric," and "Anglo-Saxon," because they strike me as some of the more ubiquitous originary moments represented in recent poetry.[32] No doubt, too, my choice of these specific originary moments reflects my own interests. The term "Sumerian" refers to poems that take ancient Sumer and related neighboring cultures, such as that of the Hittites, as an originary moment. "Homeric" refers directly to the two touchstone poems attributed to the classical poet, the *Odyssey* and the *Iliad*. "Anglo-Saxon" refers to poems that take pre-Conquest England as the focus for their engagement with the past. I will address some well-known, and some lesser-known, poems in each category in this chapter.

Of course there are other originary moments that could have been my focus here. For instance, a search for Celtic origins punctuates works by Hugh MacDiarmid, David Jones, and Seamus Heaney. A concentration on Paleolithic cultures appears in Clayton Eshleman's *Placements* series (1970s). Nathaniel Mackey's African-based *Song of the Andoumboulou* (1990s) incorporates non-Western cultural perspectives. Peter Riley's *Distant Points* (1995) examines ancient England, particularly the earthen mounds built in prehistory which dot the British landscape. On the other hand, poems that look back to the Renaissance are common in twentieth-century poetry, and it could be construed as yet another originary moment. Among postmodern poems, Kenneth Koch's *Seasons on Earth* (1987), with its heavy debt to Ariosto, and Armand Schwerner's *Cantos from Dante's Inferno* (2000) fit into this category. The task of searching for works that engage origins in twentieth-century poetry is virtually endless, and clearly not all the long poems that engage origins can be placed neatly—or at all—into the three categories I have created. Nevertheless, it is my hope that the discussion that follows will provide a sense of the variety of poems engaged in originary pursuits, even if I confine my discussion to three specific origin points.

Sumerian

The literature and culture of ancient Mesopotamia, especially Sumer, has exerted a surprising influence on writers of the long poem. Surprising because of our relatively recent acquisition of knowledge of Sumer: its existence was unknown prior to the nineteenth century, and many of its important texts—most notably *The Epic of Gilgamesh*—received wider currency only in the last century. In fact, translations of Sumer's texts have proliferated over the past few decades, with one notable version of *Gilgamesh* coming from novelist and critic John Gardner (1984). Gardner even incorporated Sumerian elements into his novel *The Sunlight Dialogues* (1972). Among poets, Ted Hughes included an imitation of Sumer's cuneiform stone tablets in *Crow* (1970), his sequence based on alternative creation myths. Hughes's poem is instructive because it offers a sense of how Sumer has been viewed: as a civilization at the beginning of recorded time and history, fundamental even if its importance as an originary moment had not been identified earlier. The title of a book by perhaps the best known Sumerologist, Samuel Noah Kramer, sums up the notion operative in these works: *History Begins at Sumer*.

Sumer's influence on the long poem is especially strong in the second wave of modernists, particularly in the work of Louis Zukofsky and Charles Olson. Written over an almost fifty-year span

"*Returning to the Origin and Bringing Something Back*"

and divided into twenty-four parts of varying length, Zukofsky's "A" (1978) remains one of the touchstone texts of late-modernist literature. Most relevant here is "A-23" which is composed of a section that translates *The Epic of Gilgamesh*. True to Zukofsky's recondite verse style, however, it is very difficult to follow the narrative thread of this rendering of the story. Zukofsky's poem is filled with word play ("Praise! gill..gam..mesh.."[33]) and the poet even changes the name of the protagonist to "Strongest" and his companion Enkidu to "One Kid." In *Louis Zukofsky and the Poetry of Knowledge*, Mark Scroggins argues that "for the most part the reader is hard-pressed to find the principle of continuity in [the] baffling but sonically exquisite lines [of "A-23"]."[34] A short excerpt from Zukofsky's text, where Gilgamesh and Enkidu are united, confirms Scroggins's insight:

> The Strongest threw him: their
> friendship sealed. Strongest to Stronger:
> "my heart weighs my lot,
> if 2/3-God must die weal's
> beyond rancor; evil's unfinished I've
> seen myself corpse bloat, river
> flood-water surge my Wall–búoyed
> no more than any urbanite;
> hated I desire the forest—
> risk to come thru it,
> daring will reach my father
> have him in unmeasured Distance["][35]

The text seems a word-for-word translation, without much attempt at the kind of idiomatic rendering one is used to finding in translations produced for a wide readership. Unity here is to be found in the use of sounds that are often dissonant and foreground Zukofsky's aesthetic vision.

Indeed, as with much of Zukofsky's long poem, the key to understanding the poetics come in analogies to music, as when he writes slightly later in the poem, "by *heart-strings* 13 frets/pro-

Chapter One

pound a law of 'all'/and each fret tuned singly/salves fret or singularly frets/to salve thing to End/dissonance harmonized."[36] Zukofsky seeks to make "dissonance harmonized" in the verse that constitutes "A-23," from the staccato transliterated text that makes up the translation of *Gilgamesh* to the hints of Early Modern and mannered Elizabethan Englishes that fade in and out as the section reaches its conclusion. "A-23" moves variously from one social register of English to another in such a way as to indicate that Zukofsky sees himself using the layers of linguistic forms as a metaphor for the passage of time and the stages of history. Or, as he says at the end of the section, calling again on a metaphor of music, "consonances/and dissonances only of degree, never-/Unfinished hairlike water of notes."[37] The *Gilgamesh* text allows Zukofsky to draw a historical parallel between his own elliptical poetics and that of Sumer, thereby emphasizing the continuity of modern verse with that of antiquity.

A fascination with ancient Sumer and its environs finds its way into the work of Charles Olson. Olson's long work *The Maximus Poems* (1983) is largely synthetic, as Pound's *Cantos* was before it, drawing together influences from cultures from all over the world. Within *Maximus*, one finds classical as well as pre-Greek civilizations depicted. Olson remarks that "the writing and acts which I find bear on the present [situation] are (I) from Homer back, not forward."[38] The "forward" Olson speaks of here is subsequent history, especially the entrenched Humanism bolstered by the Enlightenment. Olson feels mid-century American culture has reached an impasse, especially with the encroachment of commercialism and commodified popular culture, and can be remedied only by a return to modes of thinking and living characteristic of earlier cultures. The Sumerian is one of these,[39] and in *The Maximus Poems* Olson wonders:

> (where did the Sumerians
> come from, into the Persian
> Gulf—sea-peoples
> who raided and imposed themselves

"Returning to the Origin and Bringing Something Back"

> on a black-haired previous people
> dwelling among reed-houses
> on flooded marshes?[40]

Olson's translation of the Hittite "Song of Ullikummi," although not a part of *Maximus* proper, has parallels in *Maximus* and reveals Olson's mission to represent different cultures within his poem. I will return to this poem, and *Maximus*, in chapter 2.

In contrast to Olson's attempt to return to a number of originary moments—whether they are pre-Greek, specifically Sumerian, or others such as Algonquin—Armand Schwerner's *The Tablets* (1999) adopts a more skeptical point of view. In fact, *The Tablets* stands as a foil to Olson's *Maximus Poems*. Schwerner takes the work of Samuel Noah Kramer, whom Olson also read, as the point from which the underlying methods of, and motivations behind, scholarship could be critiqued. Through a series of faux translations of cuneiform tablets, Schwerner represents—albeit in a heightened way—some of the problems of scholarship and its attempt to engage past cultures. Schwerner's poem is thus largely concerned with the problems of knowing and understanding the past. Chapter 2 will be devoted to analyzing the instructive contrast of Olson and Schwerner; together they offer a particularly clear view of the way the modernist search for origins has been reinterpreted in postmodernist poetics.

The work of Judy Grahn, whose long poem *The Queen of Wands* (1982) and its companion play *The Queen of Swords* (1987) will form the basis of chapter 5, holds affinities with Schwerner's insofar as Grahn also seeks to question the assumptions of modernism. Instead of parodying scholarly conventions, however, Grahn views Sumer and its culture as a historical moment prior to the advent of the patriarchal tradition that marks Western culture. Grahn's concern, in other words, is with Sumer as a cultural origin, and despite what we might imagine as an irreconcilable difference with Olson's patriarchal persona, she agrees with the elder poet that a return to a state of mind which she detects in ancient Sumer can undo some of the historical injustices that are part of

Chapter One

our cultural inheritance. An emphasis on Grahn's self-conscious fabrication of an origin based in Sumerian culture will form the focus of chapter 5. Sumer has thus emerged as a fresh start of sorts for writers like Grahn and Olson who feel the classical tradition impeded Western civilization. It proves an alternative originary moment that predates Greece, and it is precisely this "original earliness"—to borrow a phrase from Wallace Stevens—that recommends it for these writers.[41]

Homeric

Since antiquity, Homer's epic poems the *Odyssey* and the *Iliad* have been touchstone texts in Western literature; the importance of the classical epic to Western notions of poetry and narrative is almost immeasurable. Among the literature of the twentieth century, a number of long poems use Homeric themes or poetics as major motifs or generative devices. Ezra Pound's *The Cantos*, for instance, opens auspiciously by evoking a crucial moment from the *Odyssey*. Pound's first canto is unique, however, because it is a translation of a sixteenth-century Latin version of Homer rendered by Andreas Divus. Through this approach, Pound signifies that language and time have intervened between him and his source (Homer), and he thus demonstrates the historical distance that separates the modernist poet from the origin.

An engagement with Homeric poetics persists throughout modernist literature, not only among writers of the so-called modern verse epic[42] like Pound, Williams, and Olson, but also in more lyric-driven writers like H. D.—Pound's early fellow Imagist. H. D.'s *Helen in Egypt* (1961) is an intriguing rewrite of the story of the *Iliad* from Helen's point of view. Building on the alternative tradition that Helen resided in Egypt during the events chronicled in the *Iliad*, H. D. produces a text that not only foregrounds the point of view of its female protagonist—a notion clearly distinctive among modernist long poems—but creates a work that will become important for many later female writers. As Lynn Keller implies in her survey of long poems by women, H. D. can be

"Returning to the Origin and Bringing Something Back"

viewed as one of the pioneers of the female revision of the male-dominated long poem.[43]

Helen in Egypt consists of a series of short dramatic monologues punctuated by the interpolations of an unidentified narrator. Early on, the poem centers on Helen as "Helena, Helen hated of all Greece" who is described as "the chosen, the flower // of all-time, of all-history."[44] Significantly, H. D. repeatedly imagines Helen as text: "[Helen] herself is the writing" the poem says.[45] This metaphor of textuality emphasizes the way women have been inscribed by male poetics throughout the ages. Even the narrator appears incredulous at times, remarking,

> Is this Helen actually that Helen? Achilles seems grudgingly to apologize for his first boorishness, "I was afraid." Who indeed would not be, at sudden encounter with the admitted first-cause "of all-time, of all-history."[46]

Central to the poem is Helen's agency in a war that is claimed to be waged for her sake. Achilles bitterly wonders, "[S]he could leave by a secret gate,/and the armies be saved; // why does she hold us here?"[47] Thus *Helen in Egypt* can be read as an illustration of the manner in which a woman is made the subject of a conflict she is perceived to control but in fact is only subsumed by. Judy Grahn uses H. D.'s poem as the starting point for producing her own story of women's history. I will return to this issue in chapter 5.

More recently, Louise Glück has employed the narrative framework of the *Odyssey* as a means for exploring contemporary domestic life. In *Meadowlands* (1996), Glück places Homer's characters into archetypical familial roles. The poem interweaves two narrative strands: a contemporary domestic crisis that leads to the isolation of its two protagonists and the *Odyssey* story itself that is similarly marked by domestic strain. "Nothing/is always the answer; the answer/depends on the story," the poem stresses.[48] Indeed, as the story of Odysseus, Telemachus, and Penelope becomes conflated with that of two unnamed contemporary individuals in the poem, Glück's poem pulls the *Odyssey* into the present by focusing on current marital issues. It also boldly critiques Homer's poem for its lack of interiority and sensitivity to gender-based concerns.

This critique is apparent in the poem when the Greek soldiers wait on the beach outside the walls of Troy. The speaker declares,

> these
> are men of action, ready to leave
> insight to the women and children.
> Thinking things over in the hot sun, pleased
> by a new strength in their forearms, which seem
> more golden than they did at home, some
> begin to miss their families a little,
> to miss their wives, to want to see
> if the war has aged them. And a few grow
> slightly uneasy: what if war
> is just a male version of dressing up,
> a game devised to avoid
> profound spiritual questions?[49]

The uneasy feelings that dawn on the men are presumably the "insights" they had left earlier to the "women and children." The notion that war is potentially "a male version of dressing up" is obviously critical of the male-centered violence one finds especially in the *Iliad*, a poem whose initial lines announce its subject as Achilles' "rage."[50] In this way, Glück is able to repudiate the male- and war-centered tradition of the predecessor of the long poem, the epic, even as she appropriates elements of the ancient epic to examine issues of much interest today such as the dynamics of gender constructions.

Other recent work with Homer includes Christopher Logue's translation of the *Iliad* as *War Music* (1997). Logue's poem makes liberal use of anachronisms.[51] These historical dislocations often update Homer's original epic similes. For instance, in an altered version of a famous scene from the *Iliad* in which Achilles addresses his horses, Logue describes the power of the horses pulling the chariot:

> The chariot's basket dips. The whip
> Fires in between the horses' ears.
> And as in dreams, or at Cape Kennedy, they rise,
> Slowly it seems, their chests like royals, yet
> Behind them in a double plume the sand curls up,
> Is barely dented by their flying hooves,
> And wheels that barely touch the world,
> And the wind slams shut behind them.[52]

The simile of Cape Kennedy is strikingly anachronistic, yet it seems an appropriate image, a fitting contemporary analogue, for the wonder of a world in which a god can imbue an animal with the faculties of speech and limitless brute power. Logue's poem argues for the timelessness of Homer's text; that is, that it contains stories that speak to generations, indeed centuries, of humanity. His translation testifies to the belief that by reinvigorating Homer, the original epic poems can be made even more relevant to the present era.

Logue's unorthodox approach carries into the way he handles religion in his poem. In fact, Zeus's place within *War Music* as "God," in a monotheistic sense, proves one of the poem's innovations. This occurs when Zeus is evoked by a parody of the Christian "Lord's Prayer" by Achilles: "*Our Father, Who rules in Heaven,/Because Your will is done where will may be/Grant me this prayer.*"[53] Through strategies such as this, the text produces in present-day readers a great sympathy with the religious systems of the ancient Greeks. The text makes them mirror us so we can better understand the characters' motivations. Logue's text points to the continuity of human worship, even if the supplication clearly parodies Christian conventions.

Derek Walcott, winner of the Nobel Prize in Literature (1992), has also extensively reworked Homeric texts in his play *The Odyssey* (1993) and in his long poem *Omeros* (1990). *Omeros* will receive

Chapter One

specific treatment in chapter 3. Suffice it to say now that Walcott views the conflict in Homer's *Iliad* as analogous to the tensions that pervade his native Caribbean island of St. Lucia, which was at the center of a long colonial struggle between England and France. Walcott's narrative recasts Homer's characters while also producing figures of its own: its narrator becomes a major actor in the story, as does Homer himself as a transformed figure. In the chapter to follow, I will look into the ways in which the intense self-reflexivity employed by Walcott qualifies his postcolonial reading of Homer. Hence an interest in Homer, a juggernaut of Western literature, persists into the work of a postcolonial thinker like Walcott who finds he must somehow contend with Homer's precedence—his originary presence. This struggle testifies to the enduring influence of the Homeric epics on contemporary writers of the long poem.

Anglo-Saxon

In twentieth-century poetics, Pound's 1911 translation of the Anglo-Saxon "lyric" "The Seafarer" might be considered the starting point for Anglo-American literary interest in England's early, pre-Conquest period.[54] Pound famously (and purposefully) mistranslates one line of the poem as "'mid the English" (it is usually rendered "among the angels") and in this way implies an argument for the importance of the "English" literary tradition.[55] He notes that "The Seafarer" and *Beowulf* are examples of an "indigenous art," "an art not newly borrowed."[56] W. H. Auden follows Pound with a version of another Anglo-Saxon lyric, "The Wanderer," in 1930. Like Pound, who feels the second half of "The Seafarer" is a later, Christian addition, Auden produces a rather truncated version of the medieval poem.[57] These poets believe they are returning the texts to a more "original" state, free from the accumulations of later ages. Pound also notably applies an Old English–inspired alliterative verse style to the opening of his *Cantos*. In this way, he synthesizes classical and medieval influences in his influential long poem and invites later poets to utilize "origins" to their own ends.

"Returning to the Origin and Bringing Something Back"

In other long poems, Anglo-Saxon themes and poetics make intriguing appearances. I have already noted that David Jones's *The Anathemata: Fragments of An Attempted Writing* (1952) integrates Anglo-Saxon and Welsh sources. Jones also reimagines other cultures of antiquity, such as the Roman Empire, in his poetry. Jones's strategy recalls Pound's mixture of diverse cultures. Anglo-Saxon culture takes precedence in *The Anathemata*, however, as Jones liberally peppers his work with Old English terms and employs a verse style that often gestures toward the medieval alliterative verse tradition. Occasionally Jones even introduces echoes of Anglo-Saxon texts into his poem, as when he writes, "for 'tis to garnish paps/that nourish such as must strike soundings in the gannet's bath." A note he supplies advises, "See *Anglo-Saxon Chronicle* under A.D. 973, ' . . . over the rolling waters, over the gannet's bath, . . . over the water's throng, over the whale's domain.'"[58] As with many other twentieth-century long poems, *The Anathemata* generates a sense of accumulated human culture and history through its methods of quotation and allusion; the long poem is the receptacle to hold these separate shards of the past together. Jones goes further than even Pound or Zukofsky in assuring the reader understands his references by producing a preface that delineates his methods and footnotes that catalog his sources, as the example illustrates. His approach contrasts with Armand Schwerner's skepticism about scholarly methods; in fact Schwerner's poem might be read as a postmodern parody of the conventions utilized in texts such as Jones's.

Basil Bunting's verse style, especially as it appears in his long poem *Briggflatts* (1966), has been recognized as widely influential on later British poets.[59] In Bunting's poem, the passage of time is a major motif:[60] "Then is Now," the poem says repeatedly.[61] Bunting emphasizes the present moment's continuity with the past and shows how the two can occupy the mind at precisely the same time, as Pound argues in his phrase used by Rothenberg's anthology ("[a]ll ages are contemporaneous in the mind"). Bunting evokes the figure of Eric Bloodaxe, whom he stresses "Northumbrians should know . . . but seldom do, because all the school histories are written by or for southrons."[62] He suggests, "Piece his story together from the Anglo-Saxon Chronicle, the Orkneyinga Saga, and Heimskringla, as you fancy."[63] These historical allusions are developed concurrently with the life of the poem's protagonist who is characterized as "sick, self-maimed, self-hating,/obstinate, mating/beauty with squalor to beget lines still-born."[64] The poem is thus a kind of palimpsest in which the present of the protagonist is written over the past (Eric Bloodaxe and the Anglo-Saxon themes), which consistently remains visible in the text.

The music of Bunting's poem recalls Anglo-Saxon verse in its syntax and alliterativeness: "Who sang, sea takes,/brawn brine, bone grit./Keener than kittiwake./Fells forget him./Fathoms dull the dale,/gulfweed voices . . ." one stanza reads.[65] Bunting's verse style performs a function similar to that observable in the works of Olson and Zukofsky: the aesthetic effect recalls the cultures which are themselves the subjects of the poems. In other words, this is a kind of double approach to engaging or recalling an originary moment as the literary form (alliterative verse) is intended to signify the past culture (Anglo-Saxon). But as with Olson or Zukofsky, Bunting does not wish to employ a medieval verse form slavishly; instead he transforms the ancient poetics into a modern idiom so that the present frames the past.

The Irish Nobel Prize winner (1995) Seamus Heaney has consistently engaged the Anglo-Saxon past of Great Britain in his work. Heaney's view, however, is far more conflicted than Jones's or Bunting's. W. B. Yeats anticipated Heaney's ambivalence when he remarked, "Gaelic is my national language, but it is not my mother tongue."[66] In a short poem from early in his career, "Belderg," Heaney similarly notes the tension that informs his use of language:

> I'd told how its foundation
>
> Was mutable as sound
> And how I could derive
> A forked root from that ground

"Returning to the Origin and Bringing Something Back"

> And make *bawn* an English fort,
> A planter's walled-in mound,
>
> Or else find sanctuary
> And think of it as Irish,
> Persistent if outworn.[67]

The foundation is likened to sound and the importance of the English language is questioned in face of the Irish term "bawn." This poem comes from Heaney's volume *North* (1975)—a book that contains part of his discontinuous series of "Bog poems" which constitute their own kind of long poem. In his reliance on language to imply political conflict—"bawn" and the "English fort"—Heaney begins a process which reaches its latest phase in his translation of *Beowulf* (2000).

In *North*, Heaney writes of a wish to "come past/philology and kennings," but he finds himself back among those kennings when he begins a translation of *Beowulf* at the request of the editors of *The Norton Anthology of English Literature*.[68] In describing his translation, Heaney employs a metaphor of excavation that appears often in *North*.[69] He speaks of "a strong desire to get back to the first stratum of the language," that is, the writings of the Anglo-Saxons.[70] "I consider *Beowulf* to be part of my voice-right," Heaney declares, but he also recounts the cultural friction he experiences in approaching the first English epic as a Catholic-raised poet from Northern Ireland.[71] Language again turns out to be Heaney's means of critique and resistance. He speaks of his use of the word "bawn" in his translation as a way of placing his own linguistic politics into the poem. "Putting a bawn into *Beowulf*," Heaney writes, "seems one way for an Irish poet to come to terms with that complex history of conquest and colony, absorption and resistance, integrity and antagonism."[72] Heaney exhibits his consciousness of political history through the only means available to him as a poet: language.

Geoffrey Hill's work represents a more historically-conscious British poetry than that of Jones or Bunting. Hill's long poem

Chapter One

Mercian Hymns (1971) and what I would consider its complementary poem, "An Apology for the Revival of Christian Architecture in England," constitute the case-study chapter on the Anglo-Saxon (chapter 4). Hill emerges as a poet who feels he must self-consciously engage England's history in a way that is difficult to discern among poets from earlier in the century. Like Heaney, Hill questions Britain's imperial past and ponders the significance of the events in Britain's turbulent history. Chapter 4 will focus on Hill's interrogation of notions of the nation as they are figured in originary thinking. Through the process of reflecting on Britain as a nation, Hill responds to his literary predecessors such as Pound and Bunting who see Anglo-Saxon England as indispensable to an understanding of the origin of the modern nation. Hill's postmodern dubiousness of the assurance of Pound and Bunting represents a clear case of a modernist point of view undergoing revision by a postmodernist.

The Case-Study Chapters

I have shown that a preoccupation with the three originary moments I have identified—Sumerian, Homeric, and Anglo-Saxon—cuts across a number of writers over the course of the last century. The obvious advantage of examining poems concerned with origins is that it permits us to reflect on a collection of otherwise disparate poets, poets with agenda sometimes at odds with one another who nevertheless all engage in a consideration of the past's continuity with the present.

Before going on to further delimit the reasons why the poets have been chosen for each case-study chapter, first I should emphasize that in choosing these writers, I do not seek to make arguments for each poet's relative worth—for instance, that Geoffrey Hill's poetry holds the same aesthetic value as Judy Grahn's, or vice versa. Of course, to some degree, including these particular poets in this book implies their work deserves serious study. Still, I do not see my function here as creating or reinforcing canons so much as presenting a sense of the breadth of writers who engage the originary moments I have indicated.

Having said that, I should note that the writers chosen for closer examination represent a diversity of identity—Schwerner a Jewish-born American turned Buddhist; Walcott a Caribbean writer of "mixed" ancestry;[73] Hill a canonical British poet; Grahn an American-born lesbian—which is important for showcasing the range of poets engaged in originary pursuits. Additionally, these poets differ considerably in their approaches to origins and these differences are significant and instructive. Schwerner is engaged in a project to parody the modernist search for origins. Walcott questions the veracity of the European tradition that finds its origin in Homer. Hill examines the logic of seeing Anglo-Saxon England as the origin of the modern British nation. Grahn seeks to revise the search for origins to feminist ends. Their long poems were all published in the latter decades of the century and sit comfortably—historically speaking—within postmodernity (Schwerner's between 1968 and 1999, Hill's poems from the '70s, Grahn's from the '80s, and Walcott's from 1990). Even though these poems are quite different in local ways in their relationship to origins, they are engaged in a process of literary dialogue that continues modernism's inquiry into the past.

These writers also introduce specific themes within the larger issue of the search for origins: the construction of national identity (in the case of Hill), the processes of literary revisionism (with Olson and Schwerner), the influence a search for origins wields in postcolonial thinking (in Walcott), and the way women writers have sought to create a new tradition within the context of patriarchally based culture (as Grahn does). Thus, I feel these poets address a number of issues of much interest to literary studies today, and this too recommends them as excellent candidates for analysis. Through the case-study chapters, I broach issues of importance in modernism (for instance, in chapter 5 I address the modernist penchant for myth and the modernist anxiety of leakage between high and low cultures) and illustrate some of the ways in which

Chapter One

postmodernists have addressed modernist concerns. I begin my case studies with the works of Olson and Schwerner because of their instructive illustration of the shift from late-modernist to postmodernist viewpoint. Let us now look closer at these poems.

Endnotes

1. By "originary moments," I mean specific cultures or historical periods from which poets contend our present culture descends.
2. Octavio Paz, *The Other Voice: Essays on Modern Poetry* (New York: Harcourt Brace Jovanovich, 1991), 7.
3. Whitman is usually seen as the source of the modern long poem. Roy Harvey Pearce noted in 1961 that Whitman created "an American equivalent of an epic" (*The Continuity of American Poetry* [Princeton: Princeton University Press, 1961], 83). Jeffrey Walker in *Bardic Ethos and the American Epic Poem* (Baton Rouge: Louisiana State University Press, 1989) analyzes the rhetorical tradition initiated by Whitman, and its effect on later poets. Thomas Gardner, in *Discovering Ourselves in Whitman: The Contemporary American Long Poem* (Urbana: University of Illinois Press, 1989), chronicles Whitman's influence on a number of contemporary poets, such as James Merrill and John Ashbery.
4. Joseph Conte has examined the long poem as it appears among more experimental writers such as these in *Unending Design* (Ithaca: Cornell University Press, 1991). He abandons the term "long poem" and instead decides to speak of "serial" and "procedure" forms, which he notes are "strictly postmodern innovations" (3). The narrowness of his focus makes it difficult to apply his terms to this study. The lyrical aspect of the long poem has been analyzed by Charles Altieri in a special issue of *Genre*. He writes, "The most distinctive feature of the modernist long is the desire to achieve epic breadth by relying on structural principles inherent in lyric rather than narrative modes" ("Motives in Metaphor: John Ashbery and the Modernist Long Poem," *Genre* 11.4 [Winter 1978], 653). Similarly, M. L. Rosenthal and Sally Gall have traced the lyrical influence on a number of long poetic works over the course of the last century and a half in their

"Returning to the Origin and Bringing Something Back"

book *Modern Poetic Sequence: The Genius of Modern Poetry* (New York: Oxford University Press, 1986).

5   I should note that the literature on origins in poststructuralist thought, which informs my understanding of the concept here, is deep. Edward W. Said accentuates the difference between a "beginning" and an "origin" by noting that the "latter [is] divine, mythical and privileged, the former secular, humanly produced, and ceaselessly re-examined" (*Beginnings: Intention and Method* [New York: Columbia University Press, 1985], xii–xiii). The classic poststructuralist text for theories of origins, however, is undoubtedly Jacques Derrida's *Of Grammatology*, where Derrida speaks of "the myth of the origin" and shows how origins are never stable, natural, but are always constructed (*A Derrida Reader*, ed. Peggy Kamuf [New York: Columbia University Press, 1991], 52). Derrida's thinking has been extended by Judith Butler who applies the concept to gender theory in her article "Imitation and Gender Insubordination." She notes, "[T]he entire framework of copy and origin proves radically unstable as each position inverts into the other and confounds the possibility of any stable way to locate the temporal or logical priority of either term," (*Literary Theory: An Anthology*, eds. Julie Rivkin and Michael Ryan [Malden, MA.: Blackwell, 1998], 723).

6   Seamus Heaney, *Poems: 1965–1975* (New York: Noonday, 1988), 195.

7   Margaret Dickie, *On the Modernist Long Poem* (Iowa City: University of Iowa Press, 1986), 162.

8   Dickie, *Modernist Long Poem*, 6. While reading Dickie's book, one might form the impression that the long poem is exclusively the territory of male writers. However, scholars have recently reevaluated the use of the genre by women. Susan Stanford Friedman identifies "four self-authorizing strategies" women adopt in using the form—"the ironist, historicist, re-visionist, and experimentalist"—in their attempts to "feminize the genre" ("When a 'Long' Poem is a 'Big' Poem: Self-Authorizing Strategies in Women's Twentieth-Century 'Long Poems,'" *LIT* 2 [1990], 12; 21). Judy Grahn, the poet I study in chapter 5, occupies Friedman's second category, "the re-visionist," in my view. In her book devoted to women's long poems, *Forms of Expansion: Recent Long Poems by Women* (Chicago: University of

Chicago Press, 1997), Lynn Keller writes that "precisely because [the long poem] has been so dominated by men, [it] offers—as genres like the novel or lyric, say, cannot—unusually unobstructed perspectives for viewing women's interactions with male-dominated traditions" (16–17).

9 Origin-seeking is observable in Middle English poems such as *Sir Gawain and the Green Knight* (ca. 1370) and Layamon's *Brut* (ca. 1205), which both recall Geoffrey of Monmouth's *The History of the Kings of Britain* (ca. 1137) in positing the origin of England in the figure of Brutus, great-grandson of Aeneas. In the tradition of the English "epic," a line can be traced from Edmund Spenser's *Fairie Queene* (1596) to John Milton's *Paradise Lost* (1667) to Alfred, Lord Tennyson's *Idylls of the King* (1859), which represents an inquiry into the past to divine the origin of the present. This is a tradition that the modernists inherit. In terms of national epic, one might also point out that Milton initially considered basing his epic on King Arthur until he abandoned the idea because of what he termed "long and tedious havoc fabled knights/In battles feigned" (*Paradise Lost* IX.30–31). This of course left the material open for Tennyson to seek origins in the Arthurian past in his *Idylls* and for the Arthurian past to be revisited by David Jones in the following century.

10 Heinrich Schliemann's uncovering of Troy in the 1870s; the discovery of the neolithic cave paintings in Altamira, Spain (1879), and Lascaux, France (1940); and the excavation of the Anglo-Saxon burial place Sutton Hoo in 1939 were all significant archaeological events. Later in this chapter, I will note the way the discovery and excavation of the ancient Mesopotamian civilization of Sumer informed the thinking of a number of poets in the twentieth century. The January 2004 edition of *Modernism/modernity* devotes itself entirely to the issue of archaeology in modernism. The effect of archaeology on the modernist literary imagination has also been examined in Brian McHale's *The Obligation Toward the Difficult Whole: Postmodernist Long Poems* (Tuscaloosa: University of Alabama Press, 2004). See McHale's fourth chapter, partly on Hill's poem which I also investigate in chapter 4.

"Returning to the Origin and Bringing Something Back"

11 The influence of the uncovering of originary places is evident in Pablo Neruda's discussion of the lost Incan city of Machu Picchu in *Canto General* (1950). Poets as diverse as W. H. Auden ("Archaeology") and William Bronk ("At Tikal") have utilized archaeological perspectives in their poetry. Seamus Heaney's work also has been deeply informed by notions of excavation. A writer I will cite later, Peter Riley, actually uses turn-of-the-century archaeological records as source material for the development of his long poem, *Distant Points* (1995). The list could go on.
12 Ezra Pound, *Personae: The Shorter Poems*, eds. Lea Beachler and A. Walton Litz (New York: New Directions, 1990), 186.
13 Pound, *Personae*, 188.
14 "Modernist literature has a deserved reputation for being radically experimental in theme, structure, and technique. And yet the more one ponders it and its successors in the century, the more its collective voice appears to speak elegiacally" (John B. Vickery, "Frazer and the Elegiac: The Modernist Connection," in *Modernist Anthropology: From Fieldwork to Text*, ed. Marc Manganaro [Princeton: Princeton University Press, 1990], 51). He notes that this "elegiac" perspective requires modernist works to present a "backward look at cultural history perceived as a sequence of receding vistas and superimpositional perspectives" (54).
15 Pound, *Personae*, 188.
16 Terry Eagleton admits a negative view of postmodernism. Although I differ considerably in my sense of the relative worth of the phenomenon, I agree with Eagleton's description of its elements. He writes that postmodernism is "depthless, decentered, ungrounded, self-reflexive, playful, derivative eclectic, pluralistic art which blurs the boundaries between 'high' and 'popular' culture, as well as art and everyday experience" (*The Illusions of Postmodernism* [Oxford: Blackwell, 1996], vii). The postmodern poems I will look at in this chapter, and especially in those chapters to follow, reveal many of the characteristics Eagleton indicates, particularly self-reflexivity, playfulness, pluralism, and the breakdown of a division between high and low cultures.

17 T. S. Eliot, *The Use of Poetry and the Use of Criticism: Studies in the Relation of Criticism to Poetry in England* (Cambridge: Harvard University Press, 1964), 111. Emphasis added.
18 Paul De Man, *Blindness and Insight: Essays in the Rhetoric of Contemporary Criticism*, 2nd ed. (Minneapolis: University of Minnesota Press, 1983), 97.
19 Blackwell's *A Concise Companion to Modernism* offers a useful overview of primitivism in modernism in its chapter on anthropology (David Bradshaw, ed. *A Concise Companion to Modernism* [Malden, MA: Blackwell, 2003]).
20 Eliot, *The Use of Poetry*, 148. Eliot's emphasis. Marc Manganaro writes on Eliot, "What fuses the 'ancient' to the 'civilised' in the poet is the very process of formulating the sound of verse, of building up 'syllable and rhythm.' That process, inherently mystical or prelogical, Eliot saw as a return to 'primitive' origins" ("'Beating a Drum in a Jungle': T. S. Eliot on the Artist as 'Primitive,'" *Modern Language Quarterly* 47.4 [December 1986], 402).
21 Marianna Torgovnick, *Gone Primitive: Savage Intellects, Modern Lives* (Chicago: University of Chicago Press, 1991), 19, 246. Torgovnick's emphasis.
22 I will look at this concept briefly in chapter 3.
23 Torgovnick, *Gone Primitive*, 245.
24 As with his earlier anthologies of the '60s and '70s, in *Poems for the Millennium* (Berkeley: University of California Press, 1995) Rothenberg favors avant-garde writers and presents the work of two poets I will analyze in chapter 2: Charles Olson and Armand Schwerner.
25 Rothenberg and Joris, *Poems for the Millennium*, 733. Rothenberg and Joris's emphasis.
26 See my article ("Anglo-Saxon and Welsh Origins in David Jones's *The Anathemata*," *North American Journal of Welsh Studies* 6.1 [Winter 2006]: 1–18) for an analysis of the tensions between Anglo-Saxon and Welsh sources in Jones's long poem.
27 Jerome Rothenberg, *Technicians of the Sacred: A Range of Poetries from Africa, America, Asia, and Oceania* (Garden City, NY: Doubleday, 1968), xix.

"Returning to the Origin and Bringing Something Back"

28 Rothenberg, *Technicians*, xix.
29 A later manifestation of the linking of origins and naming appears in the discussion of Derek Walcott's *Omeros* in chapter 3.
30 See the first chapter in Vernon Shetley's *After the Death of Poetry: Poet and Audience in Contemporary America* (Durham: Duke University Press, 1993) for an account of the distance that has grown between poetry and the culture at large as a result of the "difficulty" of modernism.
31 As chapter 5 will show, Eliot's notion of the "mythical method" is a corrective measure meant as "a way of controlling, of ordering, or giving shape and a significance to the immense panorama of futility and anarchy which is contemporary history" (T. S. Eliot, *Selected Prose*, ed. Frank Kermode [New York: Harvest, 1975], 177).
32 I should note that these categories are not equal in the sense that as many writers are engaged by Sumer or Anglo-Saxon England as by Homer; certainly the Homeric epics have exerted a larger influence over time, up to the present.
33 Louis Zukofsky, *"A"* (Baltimore: Johns Hopkins University Press, 1978), 540.
34 Mark Scroggins, *Louis Zukofsky and the Poetry of Knowledge* (Tuscaloosa: University of Alabama Press, 1998), 39.
35 Zukofsky, *"A,"* 540–41.
36 Zukofsky, *"A,"* 558.
37 Zukofsky, *"A,"* 563.
38 Charles Olson, *Collected Prose*, ed. Donald Allen and Benjamin Friedlander (Berkeley: University of California Press, 1997), 207.
39 John Maier analyzes the use of Sumerian themes in Olson's non-Maximus poems in the book he edits, *Gilgamesh: A Reader* (Wacuonda, IL: Bolchazy-Caduci Publishers, 1997).
40 Charles Olson, *The Maximus Poems*, ed. George F. Butterick (Berkeley: University of California Press, 1983), 275.
41 Wallace Stevens, *Collected Poetry and Prose*, ed. Frank Kermode and Joan Richardson (New York: Library of America, 1997), 410.
42 The term is from Michael André Bernstein's book *The Tale of the Tribe: Ezra Pound and the Modern Verse Epic* (Princeton: Princeton University Press, 1980). Bernstein demonstrates how poems by

Pound, William Carlos Williams, and Olson revivify elements of the epic tradition.

43 Keller, *Forms of Expansion*, 16.
44 H. D., *Helen in Egypt* (New York: New Directions, 1961), 2; 20.
45 H. D., *Helen*, 22.
46 H. D., *Helen*, 47. H. D.'s emphasis.
47 H. D., *Helen*, 49.
48 Louise Glück, *Meadowlands*, (Hopewell, NJ: Ecco, 1996), 9.
49 Glück, *Meadowlands*, 14.
50 Homer, *The Iliad*, trans. Robert Fagles (New York: Penguin, 1990), 77.
51 Anachronisms form part of the analysis of Geoffrey Hill's *Mercian Hymns* (1971) in chapter four.
52 Christopher Logue, *War Music: An Account of Books 1–4 and 16–19 of Homer's "Iliad"* (New York: Noonday, 1997), 214.
53 Logue, *War Music*, 151.
54 However, Alfred, Lord Tennyson's version of "The Battle of Brunanburh" (1880) might be seen as an important forerunner.
55 Pound, *Personae*, 62.
56 Ezra Pound, *Literary Essays*, ed. T. S. Eliot (New York: New Directions, 1968), 34. His complete statement runs thus: "We may count the Seafarer, the Beowulf, and the remaining Anglo-Saxon fragments as indigenous art; at least, they dealt with a native subject, and by an art not newly borrowed. Whether alliterative meter owes anything to Latin hexameter is a question open to debate; we have no present means of tracing the debt" (34). As Hugh Kenner stresses, Pound's interests reflect his era: "The time's enthusiasm for Anglo-Saxon studies was transmitted to Pound by Professor Ibbotson at Hamilton; it led in 1911 to his Seafarer" (*The Pound Era* [Berkeley: University of California Press, 1973], 108). John Tytell points out that the genesis of Pound's long poem *The Cantos* occurs in a conversation with his Anglo-Saxon Professor: "Ibbotson . . . introduced Pound to Anglo-Saxon. It was during one of their long talks that Pound conceived the idea of a long epic poem about history that would become *The Cantos*" (*Ezra Pound: The Solitary Volcano* [New York: Anchor Press, 1987], 23).
57 Nicholas Howe analyzes Auden's place in the host of writers who examine Anglo-Saxon origins in his article "Praise and Lament: The

Afterlife of Old English Poetry in Auden, Hill, and Gunn," *Words and Works: Studies in Medieval English Language and Literature in Honour of Fred C. Robinson*, ed. Peter S. Baker and Nicholas Howe (Buffalo: University of Toronto Press, 1998): 293–310. Also notable is the recent short article by Nick Salvato in *Notes and Queries* which traces Zukofsky's debt to Old English sources for the section of *"A"* I have associated with Sumerian poetics, "A-23." "Louis Zukofsky's Old English Sources for 'A'-23," *Notes and Queries* 49.1 (March 2002): 85–88.

58 David Jones, *The Anathemata: Fragments of an Attempted Writing* (Boston: Faber and Faber, 1952), 146. Perhaps it is also a reference to "The Seafarer" in which gannets appear early in the poem.

59 See the editors' introduction to *Other: British and Irish Poetry Since 1970* for an assessment of Bunting's place in contemporary British poetry. Richard Caddel and Peter Quartermain, eds., *Other: British and Irish Poetry Since 1970* (Hanover: Wesleyan University Press, 1999), xxviii.

60 Randall Stevenson analyzes time as a major motif in modernist works in his book *Modernist Fiction: An Introduction* (Lexington: University Press of Kentucky, 1992).

61 Basil Bunting, *The Complete Poems*, ed. Richard Caddel (New York: Oxford University Press, 1994), 62.

62 Bunting, *Complete Poems*, 210.

63 Bunting, *Complete Poems*, 210.

64 Bunting, *Complete Poems*, 47.

65 Bunting, *Complete Poems*, 48.

66 William Butler Yeats, *The Yeats Reader: A Portable Compendium of Poetry, Drama, and Prose*, rev. ed. ed. Richard J. Finneran (New York: Scribner, 2002), 429.

67 Heaney, *Poems*, 169. Heaney's emphasis.

68 Heaney, *Poems*, 184.

69 See the fourth chapter of McHale's *The Obligation Toward the Difficult Whole* for a discussion of the use of archaeological motifs in Heaney.

70 Seamus Heaney, *Beowulf: A New Verse Translation* (New York: W.W. Norton, 2000), xxii.

71 Heaney, *Beowulf*, xxiv.

Chapter One

72 Heaney, *Beowulf*, xxx.
73 The speaker of Walcott's "*The Schooner* Flight" shares his author's heritage and notes, "I have Dutch, nigger, and English in me,/and either I'm nobody, or I'm a nation" (Derek Walcott, *Collected Poems: 1948–1984* [New York: Farrar, Straus and Giroux, 1986], 346).

2

Charles Olson's *The Maximus Poems* and Armand Schwerner's *The Tablets*: From Late Modernist to Postmodernist Long Poem

Schwerner's "Tablets," Parody, and Charles Olson

As a text marked by intense self-reflexivity, Armand Schwerner's *The Tablets* (1999) represents a turning point in poetics away from the works of literary giants like Eliot, Pound, and Stevens to the literature of postmodernism of the second half of the twentieth-century that employs formal play to question the epistemological assumptions of modernism.[1] With a publishing history stretching more than three decades (1968–1999), *The Tablets* derives from an experience Schwerner had during his graduate education:

Chapter Two

> The thing that spawned the beginning stages of that work occurred when I was a graduate student working in the Columbia Library. At the end of one of the long stacks I stuck out my arm to rest it on one of the shelves for a moment, looked at what I was covering and there was a large format edition of Samuel Noah Kramer's translation and transliteration from the Sumerian. I interpreted my experience as an omen. I have never forgotten the power of that initial charge. Charge in both senses, both electricity *and* the responsibility for a task I hadn't yet formulated.[2]

Yet Schwerner's work-to-come would not consist of direct translations of Sumerian texts, even though he would have a productive career as a translator of figures such as Sophocles and Dante. Instead he would complete a long poem that might have been regarded as one of the more elaborate literary hoaxes of the twentieth century if it were not for the irony that saturates the poem.[3] Consisting of a series of sections which echo the style and content of ancient Sumerian clay tablets, nowhere does the poem indicate that it is in any way disingenuous. It is only through the ironic phrases and position of its speaker, its "scholar/translator" as he calls himself, that the reader recognizes the text's parodic nature.

Indeed, the poem can be characterized as a parody of scholarly editions of translated works, particularly the versions of Sumerian texts rendered by Kramer and other scholars. Parody is often seen as a parasitic and vacuous genre, as Margaret Rose has observed. She writes that the "effects of [the] relegation of parody to the burlesque have included the development of a modern view of it as an inferior literary form, incapable of either complexity or seriousness."[4] Contrary to this point of view, Rose points out that parody can ask serious questions and in fact, as I will show, the parodic strategies of *The Tablets* call on us to question our relationship to nothing less than history itself. The poem forces us to consider how we can ever obtain a strong connection with the past when the documents we rely on—historical manuscripts, passed down in various conditions—can be plagued with modern interpolations. It asks us to consider whether there is a way to overcome the

Olson's "The Maximus Poems" and Schwerner's "The Tablets"

inherent problems of any text that is mediated by a modern consciousness such as Schwerner's scholar/translator represents.

I should note, however, that Schwerner has little interest in providing definitive answers for the questions he poses. The reason for this is not only the virtual impossibility of answering such questions, but in the implications that come with attempting to provide answers. Were he to make definitive statements, to build structure and order out of an endlessly complicated situation, Schwerner would place himself in the company of modernist poets he admires but wishes to distance himself from: Pound and Eliot, in particular.[5] In chapter 1 I noted that John B. Vickery argues for seeing modernism as sharing a "collective voice [that] appears to speak elegiacally."[6] Schwerner's reaction to modernism includes rejecting its belief that something essential was lost in the deep past. In this way Schwerner interrogates the very notion of origins.

By contrast, the elegiac mode is evident in a poet who follows Pound and Eliot but precedes Schwerner by a generation: Charles Olson. Like Schwerner, Olson attempts to engage the past by invoking archaic themes and poetics, from Sumer as well as other ancient civilizations, in his poetry. As the work of the last twenty years of his life (1950–1970), Olson's *The Maximus Poems* remains one of the influential texts of the middle of the twentieth century. Although nearly contemporary with *The Tablets*, *Maximus* utilizes a vastly different tone and is bereft of the self-reflexive irony of Schwerner's poem. Schwerner and Olson entertain very different ways of thinking about the world, ways which I believe are indicative of the philosophical shift from modernist to postmodernist viewpoints.

Thus the texts of Olson and Schwerner are the focus of this chapter for reasons central to the development of the long poem. They share much of the same territory in terms of thinking about an "archaeological" approach to the past which entails looking into ancient texts and "recovering" them for modern poetry. The poems are at odds in their views of epistemology: I have noted that Schwerner resists the urge to offer solutions to the questions he raises in his text. Olson, on the other hand, is consistently engaged in a search for answers. In the final analysis we must consider whether or not Schwerner's hesitancy to generalize helps us move beyond our problems any more than modernism's tendency toward "metanarratives" did.[7] The same questions remain, but without answers. Thus I do not wish to say that postmodernism supersedes modernism in some qualitative sense. What I do wish to do is sketch out how the two, as represented by Olson and Schwerner, respond differently to the same central question: What is our relationship to the past? Their different responses to this question offer something of a map of the shift in mid- to late-twentieth-century poetic thought.

"I Am an Archaeologist of Morning": Olson, "The Maximus Poems," and "The Song of Ullikummi"

A number of book-length studies exist on Olson, from Robert von Hallberg's insistence that Olson's constitutes a "scholar's art," to Sherman Paul's study that finally sees Olson as a formidable nature poet, from Stephen Fredman's view of Olson's connection to the Emersonian tradition, to Judith Halden-Sullivan's analysis of Olson's Heideggerian poetics.[8] Many articles have been published on Olson as well, but Olson's originary pursuits have yet to be studied at length, and I am afraid I can only skim the surface here. Suffice it to say that Olson's long poem *The Maximus Poems* is saturated with origins in multiple senses: the origins of the earth, the origins of America, the origins of Gloucester all consume the poet. Olson's originary pursuits often entail looking into myth and thinking within archaeological terms.

Indeed, mythology and archaeology are recurring motifs in Olson's work. Archaeology becomes a metaphor for the relationship with the past Olson wishes to obtain. In fact it becomes an integral part of his idea of being a poet, as he indicates in his 1952 essay "The Present is Prologue":

Olson's "The Maximus Poems" and Schwerner's "The Tablets"

> I find it awkward to call myself a poet or a writer. If there are no walls there are no names. This is the morning, after the dispersion, and the work of the morning is methodology: how to use oneself, and on what. That is my profession. I am an archaeologist of morning. And the writing and acts which I find bear on the present job are (I) from Homer back, not forward; and (II) from Melville on, particularly himself, Dostoevsky, Rimbaud, and Lawrence. These were the modern men who projected what we are and what we are in, who broke the spell. They put men forward into the post-modern, the post-humanist, the post-historic.[9]

This passage is significant for several reasons. For one, it numbers among the first recorded uses of the term "post-modern," and anticipates the "post-humanist" philosophy of poststructuralist thinkers such as Jacques Derrida. The metaphor Olson offers for the poet—"archaeologist of morning"—is well suited to the type of work he had been doing and would continue to do in *The Maximus Poems*. There is the sense here that a new beginning is dawning, a "morning" in which the poet, the "archaeologist," can recover that which has been lost; this is a "methodology" that would indicate "how to use oneself and for what." Olson's feeling is that an excavation of the past will reconstitute the individual in the world. In the essay "Human Universe" he argues that the philosophers of Greece's Golden Age, particularly Aristotle, have impeded Western thought with their emphasis on "classification" and "logic"—both of which prevent the kind of "action"-oriented existence he urges his readers to adopt in many places in his work.[10] Olson's archaeologist seeks to rectify the West's philosophical oversights through an active search for the past.

The theme of recovering that which has been lost persists throughout Olson's thinking.[11] His belief that in Western society the individual has lost touch with his or her self is only exacerbated by the modern day commercialism he witnesses homogenizing his setting of Gloucester, Massachusetts in *The Maximus Poems*. Even before *Maximus*, however, Olson's important early long poem "The Kingfishers" (1949) carries imagery that betrays a desire to "excavate" the past. This poem presents an archaeologist who comments, "I hunt among stones."[12] This phrase presents a distinctive image of the poet attempting to encapsulate the moment in which he engages the origin: his overturning of the stones for evidence of the past, the missing origin. Olson's archaeological obsessions eventually lead him to time spent living in the Yucatan in 1951 where he searched for Mayan artifacts. Fascinated with pre-Columbian cultures, his thoughts during this period were recorded in his correspondence with Robert Creeley published as *Mayan Letters* (reprinted in *Selected Writings*).

The image of Olson as archaeologist becomes one of the enduring tropes of his long poem *The Maximus Poems*. The poem consists of three separately published sections that were gathered together by George F. Butterick for the University of California Press in 1983. Archaeological imagery persists throughout the text, particularly when Olson declares, "I would be an historian as Herodotus was, looking/for oneself for the evidence of/what is said."[13] A reiteration of the phenomenological methodology which appears in his comments on Greek philosophy in the prose works "Human Universe" and *The Special View of History* resurfaces here. But as the first volume of *Maximus Poems* ends by asking "the 128 bridge/ now brings in // what,/to Main Street?" (M, 165) with the expectations that the commercialism overtaking the town will continue as time progresses, the second volume of *Maximus Poems* witnesses a sharp shift in subject matter as Olson becomes concerned less and less with the fate of Gloucester and instead focuses on larger cosmic and mythic themes. Significantly, Olson chooses an image of Gondwanaland for the cover of *Maximus Poems IV,V,VI*—"the Earth (and Ocean) before Earth started to come apart at the seams," he explains (M, 168). The continents formed into a single mass symbolize the synthesis of disparate mythological traditions that will make up the second volume of *Maximus* poems.

While Olson concerns himself with the future of Gloucester early in the poem against "those/who advertise [it]/out," in the second book more white space invades the page and the poems turn more obscure (*M*, 8). Even the threat of commercialism is sublimated and rendered in terms of historical analogy. A whole poem reads "128 a mole/to get at Tyre," for instance (*M*, 250). The Phoenician city of Tyre[14] (home of the historical Maximus) was penetrated by Alexander the Great by the construction of a "mole" or land-bridge which connected the city to the shore. In the same way that Tyre was lost so too does Gloucester seem on the brink of losing its economic and cultural independence because of the advent of Route 128 that crosses the Annisquam River to bridge Gloucester with the rest of the nation. The analogy with Tyre further reinforces Olson's role as a modern "Maximus" and gives some sense of what he sees as the result of the economic dependence of Gloucester on the nation—namely the loss of the self-sufficient fishing industry of Gloucester. Olson's argument against the assimilation of Gloucester with the United States is far more convincing here than early in the poem when he merely tells us what Gloucester should do—here he presents a tangible consequence of Gloucester's inaction. The allusion to the "origin" of the historical Maximus in Tyre lends credibility, Olson implies, to his belief that it is a dire position America finds itself in.

Maximus IV,V,VI is rich with material culled from various mythological traditions: Sumerian, Egyptian, Native American. One poem retells an Algonquin myth which is distinctly visceral in its imagery and language in Olson's rendering:

> They said she went off fucking every Sunday.
> Only she said she walked straight through
> the mountain, and who fucked her was the spirit
> of that mountain. (*M*, 192)

A striking similarity of diction exists between this poem and a Hittite translation Olson undertakes a few years later;[15] I will turn to that poem shortly. The tale of the woman and the mountain will recur twice more in *Maximus IV,V,VI*, with little variation aside from some re-lineation and the exchange of "hill" for "mountain" between them: "[T]he woman who said she went out every Sun-

Chapter Two

day/and walked right through the rock of the mountain/and on the other side she said she was fucked/by the Mountain"(*M*, 313); "[I]nto the hill went into/the hill every Sunday/went through/the face of the/mountain // and on the other side/was fucked by/the mountain" (*M*, 358). The story's treatment of uninhibited sexuality and its engagement with an animistic view of the world offers Olson an alternative to life in the modern United States.[16] His interest in these "primitive" poetics anticipates the work of Jerome Rothenberg and the "ethnopoetics" movement (with which Schwerner was associated).[17] In "Human Universe" Olson recognizes a similar freedom of the body in the native peoples of the Yucatan: "[I]t is so very beautiful how animal human eyes are when the flesh is not worn so close it chokes, how human and individuated the look comes out of a human eye when the house of it is not exaggerated," he writes.[18] The implication is that the modern state of American society forbids this freedom with the self and the flesh. It is only by looking abroad (to the Yucatan) or to the past (the prehistory of Algonquin myth) that Olson finds models for the proper way to live in the world. Olson's thinking here might remind us of postmodernism's emphasis on plurality, but his belief in the power of the origin is distinctively modernist. In this way Olson seems to occupy a middle ground, a transitional figure in a transitional period that might be called late-modernism or ultra-modernism (if one follows Charles Jencks' nomenclature[19]).

The tale of the woman and the mountain is later juxtaposed with two other Algonquin stories; they also recur in the second volume of *Maximus*. These ancient texts allow Olson entry into another time in which he believes action is taken more directly. In one of these tales a woman and a serpent appear. For Olson this calls to mind the Old Testament depiction of Eve's temptation by the serpent. Olson held a considerable interest in Jungian archetypes, a way of thinking through which he could unite his understanding of multiple cultures.[20] He writes,

>   she who met the serpent in the pond the adulteress
>   who met the serpent in the pond

Olson's "The Maximus Poems" and Schwerner's "The Tablets"

>   and was kissed
>   by him was wrapped in his
>   coils
>
>   she had to die if she could not pass, by fucking,
>   the poison
>   on if her husband would not fuck with her
>   and die if by fucking she could not get rid of the
>   poison after
>   she had fucked with the king of the pool.[21] (M, 312)

The repetition here is the poem's most striking feature. This repetition and re-lineation of the story with each turn it makes down the page mimics the method of oral transmission of tales that gave rise to this Algonquin myth in that it is subtly changing through repetition. The repeating (and alteration) of phrasing appears to be a key element of archaic verse in Olson's view. We see him reworking this strategy with the second version of the woman and the mountain story immediately following this one in *Maximus* and we find it again in his translation of "The Song of Ullikummi."

"Ullikummi" offers Olson yet another opportunity to pursue origins.[22] For Olson, Sumer was the origin of human civilization, an alternative to the Greek classicism he resisted in his prose works. He tells Creeley in *Mayan Letters*:

> until we have completely cleaned ourselves of the biases of westernism, of greekism, until we have squared away at historical time in such a manner that we are able to see Sumer as a point from which *all* "races" (speaking of them culturally, not, biologically) egressed, we do not have permission to weight the scale one way or another.[23]

Ancient Sumer and its related cultures, such as the Hittite, proves a source to be used as a new origin, beyond problematic Greece. Olson notes that "Ullikummi" was "[t]ranslated from Hurrian and Hittite at/Wyoming (N.Y.) in March, 1964, and read/at Spo-

Chapter Two

leto 1965 to honor the presence of/Mr. Ezra Pound" (*TCP*, 600). Tom Clark indicates that this is only a "free adaptation" of the original poem.[24] Olson begins his "translation":

> fucked the Mountain
> fucked her but good   his mind
>   sprang forward
> and with the rock he slept
> and into her let his manhood
>   go five times he let it go
>   ten times he let it go. (*TCP*, 600–601)

The rest of the poem repeats these lines, sometimes mixed with transliterations of the original text. It is not surprising to find Olson repeat the image of the mountain after it was used so consistently in the *Maximus* retellings of the Algonquin myth. As in *Maximus*, Olson employs an indecorous diction to mimic a past poetics. The choice of language in "Ullikummi" is apparently based on his assumption that one can be made more "active" in the world. Language is a gateway to the past: through it humanity enters that field of active living which Olson feels is so curiously absent in the modern age. Olson's assurance in language's ability to evoke the past might strike the reader as ironic given the way language is often pushed to its signifying limits in these poems.

Olson's speculative writings have led him to be called, perhaps unfairly, a "blend of eager anthropologist and crackerbarrel philosopher."[25] His texts, like Carl Sandburg's long poem *The People, Yes* (1936), stand as important historical documents of the notion that "value is perishing from the earth," because of the encroachment of commercial capitalism which threatens a homogeneity of culture which Olson, and Sandburg, deplored.[26] Olson's solution to the situation, once he realizes his resistance is futile, is to turn inward.[27] As *The Maximus Poems* comes to utilize more white space on the page, what verse is present is mythic. We have seen that for Olson mythic and archaic sources are essential to re-situating himself within the world after millennia of misguided philosophy. In *The Tablets*, Schwerner's scholar/translator will proceed on a similar assumption as Olson's narrator, projecting his own desires onto the past in attempt to find there that which has been lost. In this way Schwerner's project is nothing less than a critique of the search for origins that drives works like Olson's.

Schwerner's Scholar/Translator in "The Tablets"

I asserted earlier that Schwerner's "translations" of purported 5,000-year-old Akkadian/Sumerian texts in *The Tablets* parody the relationship with the past which figures like Olson attempt to secure. Yet Schwerner does not parody only to mock; instead he is sympathetic to concerns like Olson's, but dubious of attempts to find solutions to contemporary problems in prehistory. The general attitude of Schwerner's poem is reminiscent of the spirit that Russian critic Mikhail Bakhtin describes in his theory of carnival. In *Problems of Dostoyevsky's Poetics*, Bakhtin analyzes carnival in terms of Dostoyevsky's fiction. He writes, "Carnivalistic laughter . . . is directed . . . toward a shift of authorities and truths, a shift in world orders."[28] It is just such a shift that we find in Olson and Schwerner. Bakhtin elaborates further on carnival in his study of Rabelais—*Rabelais and His World* in the English translation. Bakhtin traces the phenomenon to the Roman Saturnalias, through Medieval folk culture, and finally to the era of his subject matter, the Renaissance. He describes carnival as "the people's second life"[29] in which "[t]he suspension of all hierarchical precedence . . . was of particular significance"; he continues, remarking, "Rank was especially evident during official feasts; everyone was expected to appear in the full regalia of . . . his position. It was a consecration of inequality. On the contrary, all were considered equal during carnival."[30] Carnival for Bakhtin, then, is a profoundly populist phenomenon, one in which "the people . . . for a time entered the utopian realm of community, freedom, equality, and abundance."[31] One could argue, of course, that Bakhtin's rather bold statements are idealizing. However, I am not as interested in the historical validity of Bakhtin's theory as I am in the spirit it describes, a spirit

Chapter Two

that persists in Schwerner's work and distinguishes it from the seriousness of modernist-inspired endeavors like Olson's.

Further along in the introduction to his Rabelais book, Bakhtin pauses to list the qualities peculiar to what he calls "the complex nature of carnival laughter." He writes,

> It is, first of all, a festive laughter. Therefore it is not an individual reaction to some isolated "comic" event. Carnival laughter is the laughter of all the people. Second, it is universal in scope; it is directed at all and everyone, including the carnival's participants. The entire world is seen in its droll aspect, in its gay relativity. Third, this laughter is ambivalent: it is gay, triumphant, and at the same time mocking, deriding. It asserts and denies, it buries and revives. Such is the laughter of carnival.[32]

The "ambivalent" laughter that Bakhtin describes is most apparent in the figure of Schwerner's scholar/translator to whom I will turn shortly. In Schwerner's hands he is a comically mistaken figure, yet he is also to be sympathized with as he searches for origins. The central importance of carnival laughter, as Bakhtin asserts continually, is the "temporary suspension of all hierarchic distinctions and barriers among men and of certain norms and prohibitions of usual life."[33] *The Tablets*, as we shall see, allow their scholar/translator to analyze the social mores and barriers which he feels inhibit modern life, even if we become aware that the view of the past the scholar/translator projects is one of his own making.

According to Bakhtin, the flattening of hierarchical boundaries allows the carnivalistic text to be marked by inversions and subversions:

> All the symbols of the carnival idiom are filled with this pathos of change and renewal, with the sense of gay relativity of prevailing truths and authorities. We find here a characteristic logic, the peculiar logic of the "inside out" (*a l'envers*), of the "turnabout," of a continual shifting from top to bottom, from front to rear,

Olson's "The Maximus Poems" and Schwerner's "The Tablets"

of numerous parodies and travesties, humiliations, profanations, comic crownings and uncrownings. A second life, a second world of folk culture is thus constructed; it is to a certain extent a parody of extracarnival life, a "world inside out."[34]

So too does Schwerner wish to dethrone the serious and question the assumptions operative in the works of modernism. How does he do this? Primarily by making the scholar/translator exhibit impulses we would associate with modernism, such as the desire to retrieve that which has been lost in the past to remedy current-day society that seems fragmented and embroiled in futility as Eliot memorably showed in modernism's most celebrated long poem, *The Waste Land* (1922).

A carnivalistic spirit pervades Schwerner's account of his own poem. In the explanatory "Tablet Journals/Divagations" section appended to the current text he remarks:

> The scholar/translator seems increasingly inclined to express aspects of his morphemalgia; it catches up with him; in *Tablet XI* following the lines "she opened her +++++++++++++++++++++++++ and never minded/she took him splayed from them to cover it," he says, "singular confusion of pronouns here. I do not know who I am when I read this. How magnificent." By the time he gets to *Tablet XXVII*, having so variously applied his will to the reduction of space between himself and his images, as if in prayerful appeals to his unreachable monotheistic god, he unwittingly backs into the will's splintering Other.[35]

Although useful for critics in establishing Schwerner' thoughts while writing *The Tablets*, these entries, like the poem itself which evokes the conventions of scholarship, contains the irony that they—either by design or not—explicate the poem in the way a critic would. In other words, these entries preempt the work we do as readers so we start at a different point in our reading than we would ordinarily. Even when a poet writes his or her own footnotes (as in the case of Eliot's notes for *The Waste Land*) we do not have a situation as complicated as Schwerner's where our "knowing" of the text is first filtered through his commentary. Because Schwerner's notes are largely interpretive (rather than descriptive as are most of Eliot's), our own interpretations are mediated by Schwerner's insights, placing our commentary within the ironic matrix of the poem itself. If the poem parodies scholarship and criticism, anything we say about the text is already implicated within the text's general irony—in a sense we are already ironized too.

The underlying "story" of *The Tablets* is the slow disintegration of the division between the scholar/translator and the ancient peoples he finds in his renditions of the stone tablets—as Schwerner intimates in his commentary on Tablets XI and XXVII, a "reduction of space between himself and his images" ensues. Like Olson's speaker in "The Kingfishers," Schwerner's scholar/translator "hunts among stones" (i.e., cuneiform tablets) literally. *The Tablets* can be read as an elegy on the scholar/translator's desperate attempt to build a consistent vision of the world as Olson endeavored to do. Thus the scholar/translator is himself a parody of the modernist "I" in the long poem. One would need only to take a quick survey of the speaking voice at the end of modernist long poems (and here Schwerner's admitted influence Ezra Pound is paradigmatic) to observe Schwerner's difference with them. Pound speaks of attempting to make *The Cantos* "cohere," about how he "tried to make a paradiso" but apparently failed;[36] or one could recall Eliot's desperate attempt to make Tiresias "unit[e] all the rest" of his diverse characters in *The Waste Land*.[37] In "Journals/Divagations" Schwerner reflects,

> Eliot and Pound structured ironic and tragic commentaries by confronting past and present. Why not go further, I thought, and recreate the past itself, in a series of subjectively ordered variations suggestively rooted in the archaic? And, more, why not augment the confusions between illusion and reality by the further invention of a scholar-translator whose fictive but oppressively present self would add a dimension of narration? (T, 134)

Olson's "The Maximus Poems" and Schwerner's "The Tablets"

A "dimension of narration" the scholar/translator does add to the tradition of the long poem; but what are the implications of this "dimension" which is arguably the earmark of Schwerner's homage to, and critique of, modernism? I would argue that were the scholar/translator not marked by irony, this would be a late-modernist poem similar to Olson's. However, the irreverent "carnival" laughter of Schwerner's poem places everything in quotation marks so that we must acknowledge the distance Schwerner creates between his own position and that of the scholar/translator.[38] The scholar/translator works as a modernist figure for Schwerner, so preoccupied with his need to connect with that which he presumes has been lost in the past that he fabricates the past itself.

The gap I have been discussing between the archaic consciousness of the authors of the ancient tablets and Schwerner's scholar/translator is most evident in one of the scholar/translator's interlineal notes in a translation of a tablet that evokes a figure called Pinitou. He reacts:[39]

> *curious; if this is the surname, or given name, of the speaker, we are faced for the first time with a particularized man, *this* man, rescued from the prototypical and generalized "I" of these Tablets. If it is *this* man, Pinitou, I find myself deeply moved at this early reality of self; if we have here the name of an unknown deity or peer of the speaker, I am not deeply moved. (T, 26. Schwerner's emphasis.)

The split between the "I" and the "Other" important to psychoanalysis finds itself dramatized here as Schwerner's narrator reacts emotively and entirely subjectively when faced with the possibility of the unknown Other he so desperately wishes to uncover in the ancient inscriptions.[40] The identity of the scholar/translator himself hinges on "discoveries" like this one: although he wishes to find, he says, an "early reality of self," what in fact he achieves is measuring the ancient by the standard of the modern. As the first Tablet announces, "All that's left is pattern," and indeed the translator ends up identifying an image of himself—the "pattern" of his own psyche—in the past (T, 13). For Olson, projecting his philosophy on an ancient Hittite poem was not problematic, but for Schwerner this approach is fraught with dangers, in a sense increasing one's distance from the past rather than decreasing it. The more one desperately searches for the origin, the more it appears to fade into the horizon.

Not surprisingly, the scholar/translator is finally bested by his own process. In Tablet VIII, his discourse breaks down entirely and he is forced to admit the precarious hold he has had on *The Tablets* all along:

> The reader who has followed the course of these Tablets to this point may find, upon looking back to Tablet I particularly, that I have been responsible for occasional jocose invention rather than strict archaeological findings. I now regret my earlier flippancy—an attitude characteristic of beginnings, a manifestation of the resistance a man often senses when he faces the probability of a terrific demand upon his life energy. Looking back myself to that first terrific meeting with these ancient poems, I can still sense the desire to keep them to myself all the while I was straining to produce these translations—desperately pushing to make available what I so wanted to keep secret and inviolable. (T, 31)

What he does "make available" is confirmation of the increasing suspicion the reader has as *The Tablets* go on: that the archaeological methodology here is an uncovering not of an archaic and a long lost civilization but instead a kind of excavation of the translator's own fragmented modern-world psyche, so desirous to get out that it imposes its will on the past indiscriminately. The level of self-consciousness in relationship to materials illustrated here is absent in the examples from Olson I have examined. Nowhere does Olson critique his own search for cultural or poetic origins in ancient Sumer and its environs as Schwerner makes his scholar/translator do. The terms of the speaker's confession—"desire," "straining," "desperately," "secret"—all hint at the drive observable in Olson to touch history in some way, if only through his own projections onto past literature. Still, Schwerner's scholar/translator appears only dimly aware of his manipulation of the past at best.

One problem with the scholar/translator's method is that he often oversteps his disciplinary boundaries, as in Tablet XIII. Here the narrator's interlineal note comments on one of *The Tablet's* speakers:

> *psychotic rant; what surprises however involves the degree of non-analogical type of reasoning, atypical personally and culturally, of the thought-modes of archaic literatures, Sumerian, Hebrew, Ugarit etc. But the author of XIII was very likely a "cured" schizophrenic looking back, intensely directed to assess her past. (*T*, 45)

"The repressed ego cries" he declares slightly further into the text (*T*, 45). The scholar/translator has little evidence for diagnosing this speaker as a "cured" schizophrenic and it strikes the reader as exceedingly anachronistic to project this modern category on an ancient figure. Even if this is a case of schizophrenia, we might well wonder how the philological training of the scholar/translator prepares him to make such a diagnosis. His eagerness to draw premature conclusions inspires little confidence in the reader. Similarly, later in the text he analyzes a fragment of verse, only to come to the conclusion that it represents "one of the earliest instances extant of the proliferating panzer mind-track of the contemporary West" (*T*, 103)—another instance of projecting possibly anachronistically modern psychological categories onto figures of the deep past.

One of the salient motifs in *The Tablets* is that of the "palimpsest"—a document which has been written on several times, with many layers of text visible. In the "Journals/Divagations" appended to the poem, Schwerner asks, "[a] Tablet: Palimpsest w/transparent paper?" and a similar idea repeats throughout the poem (*T*, 128).[41] Gèrard Genette offers an engaging poetics of the palimpsest, the whole of which I cannot engage here. One of his points, however, might be utilized profitably: "The most elegant parody, since it is the most economical, is then merely a quote deflected from its meaning or simply from its context, or demoted from its dignified status."[42] Schwerner himself quotes sections of *The Tablets* in addition to other literary or philosophical sources in the "Journals."[43] Schwerner's quotation of these texts remind us that we must be careful of how seriously we take his insights. *The Tablets* is a sort of palimpsest upon ages of scholarship. To use Schwerner's own metaphor, his "palimpsest" is an accretion of real and fanciful literary work and in the end we have only an accumulation of texts, where the "paper" itself is "transparent."

To underscore the textual nature of the scholar/translator's understanding, Schwerner pushes the typographical limits of the lacunae-filled tablet genre in Tablet X. This poem is composed of a field of crosses, periods, and circles representing "missing," "untranslatable," and "confusing" parts of the "original" tablet, respectively. The scholar/translator's interpolation "[the the]" stands as the only words of the poem (*T*, 35). This proves yet another depiction of modern scholarship's desire to wrest meaning out of the rubble of the past—"meaning" ("[the the]") is entirely invented by the scholar/translator and offers the reader little in understanding the ancient culture.

For further evidence of the increasingly problematic interpolations of the narrator, we might return to Tablet XI, the poem Schwerner himself analyzes in the quote I looked at in the beginning of my discussion of Schwerner. In an editorial note to Tablet XI, the scholar/translator declares, "[A] singular confusion of pronouns here. I do not know who I am when I read this. How magnificent" (*T*, 36). This is preceded by a number of inquires, asking "who is speaking here?," "who is the narrator?" (*T*, 36). Anxious uncertainty replaces the narrator's earlier confidence in his scholarly distance from his work observable, for instance, in his critique of Tablet VII's early translator Henrik L. whom the scholar/translator indicates worked among the "semi-darkness of

Olson's "The Maximus Poems" and Schwerner's "The Tablets"

late 19th century archaeology" (*T*, 27). Despite the scholar/translator's protests, Henrik L.'s insertion of "Lutheran religious material" such as "Jesu Kriste" in the poem models the idiosyncratic influence the scholar/translator himself has on the construction of *The Tablets* (*T*, 27; 28). In the same way the "Norwegian divine" Henrik L. produces anachronistic Christian references in Tablet VII, (*T*, 27) so too do the scholar/translator's references compromise the ancient text—but he is clearly too close to the process to fully realize it for himself.

In this context perhaps Schwerner's characterization of the poem makes sense: "The Tablets: formal games and invention give rise to substantive concerns *and* social reality" (*T*, 127. Schwerner's emphasis). Finding important philosophical and social inquiry in the ways in which we read the past in the extensive play and "games" of *The Tablets* confirms Margaret Rose's argument that parody can use its comic elements to offer serious critique, apart from merely mocking specific texts. Here modern scholarship and thought are the subject of Schwerner's play and we are forced to consider the preconceptions we carry to any historical text. We observed Olson carrying preformed ideas of ancient living to his Hittite translation and his interpretations of Algonquin legends, both of which placed emphasis on the freedom of pre-modern sexuality. The idea that sexuality is a key to more active living seems an assumption the scholar/translator shares in Tablets III through V.

Indeed, references like "my mighty penis" (Tablet III), or slightly later the "red penis" (Tablet V), proliferate (*T*, 20; 23). The following collection of lines from Tablet IV call to mind Olson's "Ullikummi" where sexuality is the central metaphor for retrieving a lost connection with the physical world:

can the man make himself
    come

like a .... cold onyx beads

can the woman come on top
    of the man?

.... dead trees

Chapter Two

when does the man sacrifice his hands?	like sheep draped in cold mud
does the man wipe her belly with sperm?	like stories about ice, about frozen wheat
does the man put good leaves under his testicles?	+++++++++ of maggots
does the man put his lips on the sheep's udder?	in the shape of a clay tablet in frost
does the man put hand and elbow in his cow's vagina?	like death in blossoms when .....
does he ram his penis into the soft earth?	like death in petrified wood. (*T*, 21)

Absent in Olson's poems is the intense self-reflexivity present here: the man is rendered in "the shape of a clay tablet." The text overtakes the man: the scholar/translator is bested by his own medium. Although Olson allows "Ullikummi's" dance down the page to foreground his medium—poetry—the self-reflexivity of Olson's work overall does not approach the level it does in *The Tablets*. The scholar/translator's introspective admission in Tablet VIII—"On occasion it almost seems to me as if I am inventing this sequence, and such a fantasy sucks me into an abyss of almost irretrievable depression, from which only forced and unpleasurable exercises in linguistic analysis rescue me"—has some bearing here (*T*, 32). Sections of *The Tablets*, like Tablet IV, seem little more than "fantasies" of the scholar/translator. His projection of a highly-charged sexuality onto ancient persons indicates a desire for a greater connection with physical reality not present in modern life—or anyway not present in his own ascetic scholarly life, which needs to be filled with penitential exercises ("linguistic analysis") to allow forgiveness of his trespasses ("fantasy" and "pleasure").

    Olson in the final, frustrated *Maximus* poems cuts a similar figure to Schwerner's scholar/translator. Olson writes, "Only my written word // I've sacrificed every thing . . . to acquire complete/

Olson's "The Maximus Poems" and Schwerner's "The Tablets"

concentration" (*M*, 473). In the same way the scholar/translator's own text overwhelms the actual tablets', in *The Maximus Poems* the speaker's voice is all that is left when attempts have failed to reconcile the speaker with the past in a satisfying way. There is a great deal of pathos with which Schwerner concludes his scholar/translator's work, indicating he sympathizes with the position that his narrator embodies. Like Olson's narrator, Schwerner's expresses his frustrated desire for knowledge: "I cannot open the inner knot. If I could get into the space between the icons I could know something" (*T*, 83). Nevertheless, Schwerner refrains from the speculation which lies at the heart of Olson's project: it is enough for Schwerner to present the problem of historical awareness. He points out the dangers of appropriating the past and the instability of history insofar as it is composed of our understanding of fractured texts like the one the scholar/translator assembles. Schwerner's skepticism and hesitation to theorize place him more firmly within the ethos of postmodernism than Olson. Olson held to the modernist assumption, so evident in works like *The Cantos*, that one could be reconciled with the past if only one could find a manner in which to engage it properly, if one could adequately identify with the origin.

In his 1969 volume of poetry *Seaweed*, Schwerner presents Tablet IX with the qualification, "[P]*resented by the scholar-translator/transmitted through Armand Schwerner.*"[44] This notion of "transmission" is noted again on the title page of the 1971 edition of *The Tablets*.[45] In the latest, and because of Schwerner's death, final version of the poem, this distinction is wholly absent; the space separating Schwerner and the scholar/translator goes unaddressed. However, the present edition of the poem includes a CD with Schwerner reading selected *Tablets*. In these recordings the division between the poet and his narrator is intriguing. It is significant the distance Schwerner will go in framing the texts so that they seem purely the product of their scholar/translator. Thus Schwerner effaces his involvement in the text; *The Tablets* seemingly (but we know better) exist without the influence of Armand Schwerner, the poet.

Chapter Two

A different situation occurs in *The Maximus Poems* where the poet's identity is asserted to a greater extent as the poem goes on. "[O]nce more drawn into the/plague of my own unsatisfying possible identity as/denominable Charles Olson" the speaker of *Maximus* intones, and we realize at this late point in the text we have heard much more of "Charles Olson" than "Maximus" (*M*, 450). In his book *Obdurate Brilliance*, Peter Baker argues that Olson and his poem are an example of a "model of exteriority" which Baker sees as an integral part of the twentieth-century long poem.[46] While many of the writers Baker discusses do efface the "I" in an effort to "exteriorize" their poems, this is not the case with Olson. If anything, Olson's personality and thinking become more of an issue as the poem moves toward its end and the particulars of the speaker's life—"my wife   my car   my color   and   myself," *Maximus*' Kurtzian final poem reads—condition our understanding of the poem (*M*, 635).

Despite Olson's many philosophical and theoretical writings which sometime ring of postmodern thinking, he ultimately holds to the modernist impulse to find that which has been lost in the past, to recover the missing origin. Much moving poetry comes out of his struggle. Schwerner, on the other hand, like many of his contemporaries, abandons the retreat into history and myth which marks modernist verse.[47] We find in Olson and Schwerner an indication of the shift in thought and worldview which divides the twentieth century. The question we must ask of Schwerner's postmodern resistance to what Jean-François Lyotard calls "metanarratives" is whether or not we can progress from the point at which he leaves us.[48] While Olson's philosophical statements often grow too audacious, too all-encompassing, they at least conjecture a way out of perpetual difficulties. The postmodern opposition to this way of thinking refuses to postulate answers, even if it does offer us useful ways of questioning our views of the world.[49] In the next chapter I will continue my analysis of postmodernism by looking into Derek Walcott's *Omeros*. I will show how this long poem struggles with one of the perceived problems of postmodernism,

Olson's "The Maximus Poems" and Schwerner's "The Tablets"

its preoccupation with self-reflexivity, as the poem seeks to achieve political ends by revising Homer within a postcolonial setting.

Endnotes

1. One finds self-reflexive playfulness used to serious ends in many long poems from the period, by poets as diverse as Geoffrey Hill (*Mercian Hymns*, 1971); James Merrill (*The Changing Light at Sandover*, 1982); and Kenneth Koch (*Seasons on Earth*, 1987); to name only a few. John Paul Tassoni's essay on postmodern play in Koch's poem has been useful in my thinking on Schwerner here ("Play and Co-Option in Kenneth Koch's *Ko, or A Season on Earth*: 'Freedom and the Realizable World!,'" *Sagetrieb* 10.1–2 [Spring–Fall 1991], 123–132). The political implications of postmodern self-reflexivity will be a matter for the next chapter; here I only want to represent how it provides Schwerner with a means by which he can signal his distance from his literary precursors.
2. Edward Foster, "An Interview with Armand Schwerner," *Talisman* 19 (Winter 1998/1999), 43. Schwerner's emphasis
3. Brian McHale explores the issue of *The Tablets* as hoax. He writes, "If *The Tablets* had been presented otherwise than as a volume of poetry, and if it had lacked any overt signs of irony (such as the over-the-top annotation to Tablet XI), we might have been disposed to classify the work as a hoax. As it is, we suspend our disbelief and classify it as fiction" ("Topology of a Phantom City: *The Tablets* as Hoax," *Talisman* 19 [Winter 1998/1999], 87).
4. Margaret Rose, *Parody: Ancient, Modern, and Post-Modern* (Cambridge: Cambridge University Press, 1993), 68.
5. I will review a statement by Schwerner on his relation to Pound and Eliot in producing his own long poem later in this chapter.
6. John B. Vickery, "Frazer and the Elegiac: The Modernist Connection," in *Modernist Anthropology: From Fieldwork to Text*, ed. Marc Manganaro (Princeton: Princeton University Press, 1990), 51.
7. Jean-François Lyotard's view of the difference between modernism and postmodernism is that the latter exhibits an "incredulity toward metanarratives" whereas the former attempts to maintain these

metanarratives (*The Postmodern Condition: A Report on Knowledge*, trans. Geoff Bennington and Brian Massumi [Minneapolis: University of Minnesota Press, 1979], xxiv). This distinction rings true of the poets under study here. As Steven Best and Douglass Kellner point out, by "incredulity toward metanarratives," Lyotard means "the rejection of metaphysical philosophy, philosophies of history, and any form of totalizing thought—be it Hegelianism, liberalism, Marxism, or positivism" (*Postmodern Theory: Critical Interrogations* [New York: Guilford Press, 1991], 165). In the case of Olson and Schwerner, we can see the latter figure turning away from the former's attachment to two principles here: history and positivism, both of which pervade Olson's thought.

8   Robert von Hallberg, *Charles Olson: The Scholar's Art* (Cambridge: Harvard University Press, 1978); Sherman Paul, *Olson's Push: Origin, Black Mountain, and Recent American Poetry* (Baton Rouge: Louisiana State University Press, 1978); Stephen Fredman, *The Grounding of American Poetry : Charles Olson and the Emersonian Tradition* (Cambridge: Cambridge University Press, 1993); Judith Halden-Sullivan, *The Topology of Being: The Poetics of Charles Olson* (New York: Peter Lang, 1991).

9   Charles Olson, *Collected Prose*, ed. Donald Allen and Benjamin Friedlander (Berkeley: University of California Press, 1997), 206–207.

10 Olson, *Collected Prose*, 156–57. In "Human Universe," Olson writes, "If there is any absolute, it is never more than this one, this instant, in action" (*Collected Prose*, 157). I should note that the *Selected Writings* version of this essay inserts "you" after "this one" (Charles Olson, *Selected Writings*, ed. Robert Creeley [New York: New Directions, 1966], 55). See also Olson's *Special View of History* (Berkeley: Oyez, 1970) for a more extended exposition of his theories.

11 In this regard, one may see Olson punning on the concept of "mourning" in his phrase "archaeologist of morning" in the sense that mourning can be seen as an attempt to recover from loss.

12 Charles Olson, *The Collected Poems, Excluding the "Maximus" Poems*, ed. George F. Butterick (Berkeley: University of California Press, 1987, 93). Hereafter cited in the text as *TCP*.

13 Charles Olson, *The Maximus Poems*, ed. George F. Butterick (Berkeley: University of California Press, 1983), 104–105. Hereafter cited in the text as *M*.

14 One might point out that Tyre figures significantly in the *Aeneid*, the first long poetic work to appropriate a search for origins.

15 The term "fuck" is of course the most striking linguistic choice in the poem. Presumably it evokes for Olson the early Anglo-Saxon stratum of the English language and is thus ancient in itself, but as the *OED* indicates, its source is uncertain. Cognates in other Germanic languages make its origin in Old English probable, however. This kind of sexual imagery is common to "primitivist" poetry, as revealed, for instance, by the excerpts from the Australian Aborigine "Goulburn Island Cycle" reprinted in Rothenberg's *Poems for the Millennium*: "Ejaculating into their vaginas—young girls of the western tribes./ Ejaculating semen, into the young Burara girls . . ./Those Goulburn Island men, with their long penes," etc. (Jerome Rothenberg and Pierre Joris, eds., *Poems for the Millennium: Volume One* [Berkeley: University of California Press, 1995], 744). We will see how this overt sexuality is parodied in Schwerner's *Tablets*.

16 A similar sentiment is evident in Judy Grahn's work, as chapter 5 will show.

17 See also Rothenberg's anthologies such as *Shaking the Pumpkin* (*Shaking the Pumpkin: Traditional Poetry of the Indian North Americas* [Garden City, NY: Doubleday, 1972]), which contains Olson's "A Myth of the Human Universe," or his more recent *Poems for the Millennium* (1995), which contains Olson's Hittite translation and a tablet from Schwerner. For a discussion of Rothenberg's initiation of the ethnopoetics movement, and for an evaluation of Schwerner's place in it, see the fourth chapter of Norman Finkelstein, *Not One of Them in Place: Modern Poetry and Jewish American Identity* (Albany: State University of New York Press, 2001).

18 Olson, *Collected Prose*, 158.

19 Charles Jencks, *What is Post-Modernism?* (London: Academy Editions, 1996), 14. Fredric Jameson, in one of the most important critical statements on postmodernism, cites Jencks's work on late-modernism and points to "poets like Olson or Zukovsky [sic]" as those "who had

the misfortune to span two eras and the luck to find a time capsule of isolation or exile in which to spin out unseasonable forms" (*Postmodernism; or, The Cultural Logic of Late Capitalism* [Durham: Duke University Press, 1991], 305).

20 For confirmation of Olson's interest in Carl Jung's work, see especially Butterick's *Guide* which lists books "positively known to have been used by Olson" (George F. Butterick, *A Guide to "The Maximus Poems" of Charles Olson* [Berkeley: University of California Press, 1980], 757). Pages 770–771 list Jung's books. In chapter 5 we will see that Jung has an impact also on the work of Judy Grahn.

21 This story is also told earlier in the text, on page 191 of *Maximus*.

22 For a critical commentary on Olson's use of Sumerian sources in other poems, see John Maier's chapter in the collection of essays he edits, *Gilgamesh: A Reader* (Wacuonda, IL: Bolchazy-Caduci Publishers, 1997).

23 Olson, *Selected Writings*, 97–98.

24 Tom Clark, *Charles Olson: The Allegory of a Poet's Life* (New York: W.W. Norton, 1991), 322. The source of Olson's translation, as Donald Allen and Benjamin Friedlander point out in their editorial notes to Olson's *Collected Prose*, is Hans Guterbock's article "The Song of Ullikummi: Revised Text of the Hittite Version of a Hurrian Myth" from *Journal of Cuneiform Studies* (1951) (450). The article contains word-for-word transliterations which surely aided Olson in his process.

25 "Modernism and Postmodernism." *Princeton Encyclopedia of Poetry and Poetics*. 3rd ed. 1993. 794.

26 Olson, *Collected Prose*, 160.

27 Don Byrd comments that *Maximus IV, V, VI* is "the book of purgation and rebirth" based on an analogy with Dante, and notes that the final book of *Maximus* "was to have been the book of paradise" (*Charles Olson's "Maximus"* [Urbana: University of Illinois Press, 1980], 59; 61). I would argue that since the third volume represents a turning inward where the name "Charles Olson" comes to occupy the space "Maximus" once did now that Olson's hope for Gloucester has proven futile, Olson has moved from the paradise of the idea in the first volume to the hell of the reality by the last book. In other words, he has in fact reversed the Dantean order.

28 Mikhail Bakhtin, *Problems of Dostoevsky's Poetics*, trans. Caryl Emerson (Minneapolis: University of Minnesota Press, 1984), 127.
29 Mikhail Bakhtin, *Rabelais and His World*, trans. Helene Iswolsky (Bloomington: Indiana University Press, 1984), 8.
30 Bakhtin, *Rabelais*, 10.
31 Bakhtin, *Rabelais*, 9.
32 Bakhtin, *Rabelais*, 11–12.
33 Bakhtin, *Rabelais*, 15.
34 Bakhtin, *Rabelais*, 11.
35 Armand Schwerner, *The Tablets* (Orono, ME: The National Poetry Foundation, 1999), 139. Hereafter cited in the text as *T*.
36 Ezra Pound, *The Cantos* (New York: New Directions, 1995), 816; 823.
37 T. S. Eliot, *The Waste Land: A Facsimile and Transcript of The Original Drafts Including the Annotations of Ezra Pound*, ed. Valerie Eliot (New York: Harvest, 1971), 148. The scholar/translator at one point even concludes that an element of one of the tablets was "probably conceived by a blind Tiresias-figure" (*T*, 77).
38 I will return to the overlap between Schwerner and his narrator at the end of this chapter.
39 One of the important features of *The Tablets* is that the scholar/translator's notes appear in the text, dividing lines of "archaic" verse. The significance of this intertextual strategy cannot be overemphasized since the writing of the translator, by his own design, takes a hierarchal presence equal to the clay tablets he claims to translate.
40 Tom Lavazzi offers a Lacanian reading of *The Tablets*, looking into its imagery of castration and the "transcendental signifier"; the poem ultimately "initiates us into a deconstructive self-reflexiveness," he believes ("Playing it Loose with *The Tablets*," *Talisman* 19 [Winter 1998/1999], 91).
41 For instance, he presents the issue of the palimpsest on page 77 of the poem.
42 Gèrard Genette, *Palimpsests: Literature in the Second Degree*, trans. Channa Newman and Claude Doubinsky (Lincoln: University of Nebraska Press, 1997), 16–17.
43 It is surely significant that the poet's name appears for the first time in

the "Journals/Divagations" section of the text, as the author Armand Schwerner is drawn into the ironic matrix of the poem the same way any given reader is.

44 Armand Schwerner, *Seaweed* (Los Angeles: Black Sparrow Press, 1969), 39. Schwerner's emphasis.

45 Armand Schwerner, *The Tablets: I–XV* (New York: Grossman Publishers, 1971).

46 Peter Baker, *Obdurate Brilliance: Exteriority and the Modern Long Poem* (Gainesville: University of Florida Press, 1991), 1.

47 We will see, however, how Judy Grahn revivifies myth to feminist ends in chapter 5.

48 See note 7 above.

49 Perhaps Hank Lazer puts it best concerning Schwerner's work in *The Tablets* (and what I take to be one of the more postmodern features of the text) when he claims, "[Schwerner] has a fundamental ethical commitment to an epistemological incompleteness and to a truthful inconclusiveness" ("Sacred Forgery and Grounds of Poetic Archaeology: Armand Schwerner's *The Tablets*," *Chicago Review* 46.1 [2000]: 142–153. Ebscohost. 14 September 2006. <http://web.ebscohost.com>).

3

"Master, I Was the Freshest of All Your Readers": Postcolonialism and Postmodern Self-Reflexivity in Derek Walcott's *Omeros*

Derek Walcott, "Omeros," and Postcolonialism

Derek Walcott's reputation was enhanced by winning the Nobel Prize for Literature in 1992 and today he remains a vital force in world literature. His work is important for many reasons, not the least of which is the position from which he speaks: as a poet coming from the small Caribbean island of St. Lucia. As he points out, the island has been called "Helen of the West Indies" because of the contests waged between England and France over its territory.[1] St. Lucia's history informs Walcott's poetry, particularly as his work examines the aftereffects of imperialism. Although the term "postcolonial" has been used in various ways, we might profitably label Walcott a postcolonial poet if we keep in mind the

Chapter Three

definition of the term offered by Ashcroft, Griffiths, and Tiffin.[2] These critics look beyond the prefix "post" in postcolonial as implying only "after-Independence" for past colonies.[3] Instead, they write, "[P]ost-colonialism is a continuing process of resistance and reconstruction" and is "based in the 'historical fact' of European colonialism and the diverse material effects to which this phenomenon gave rise."[4] It is with the thought that postcolonialism is a "continuing process" that I use the term and, as I show here, Derek Walcott's book-length poem *Omeros* (1990) directly works through issues related to European colonialism's continuing influence on St. Lucia.

There is another side to Walcott's work which also begs attention, aside from the exposition of imperialism and colonialism that dominates many of its pages. I am thinking of the playful, self-reflexive aspect of many of his poems and plays. John Thieme writes, "Much of [Walcott's] work is metaliterary, a self-conscious discussion of the problematics of Caribbean writing and an attempt to evolve suitable forms for the rendition of his own Caribbean experience."[5] The play between artifice and content in Walcott's work will be my focus as I look into the ways in which self-reflexivity qualifies Walcott's critique of the European and African origins of St. Lucia in *Omeros*. Ultimately Walcott must resist originary thinking because it does not offer a way for the island to move forward. In fact, the one character in the poem who remains willfully preoccupied with origins, Achille, shows the smallest personal growth by the close of the book.

Omeros reinvents Homer's epics within a Caribbean setting. This process of revivifying older texts exists throughout Walcott's oeuvre, such as in his transformation of the Don Juan story in *The Joker of Seville* (1974) and in his Caribbean-influenced stage version of *The Odyssey* (1993). At once both an homage and a subversion, *Omeros* is ambivalent about its precursor texts: elements of the original works persist within Walcott's poem, but with consistent adjustments and reconfigurations.[6] The narrator of *Omeros*, who also happens to be one of its major characters, feels the primary figures of the *Iliad*—Hector, Achilles, Helen—offer him a means for describing the social friction of St. Lucia. Yet he is also dubious of the historical legacy of empire that influences the actions of these characters in his poem. The narrator draws parallels between Homer's ancient poems and his own, not only in the characters they share but also in the way they work with themes of social contest and foreign occupation. The *Iliad*, especially, stands in Walcott's thinking as a "poem of force," as Simone Weil memorably calls it.[7]

In *Omeros* Homer represents the legacy of the West haunting writers like Walcott who have been both marginalized and influenced by European literature. The quotation that forms part of my chapter title, which the poem's narrator addresses to the figure of Homer, alludes to this situation: "Master, I was the freshest of all your readers."[8] I will turn to the relationship between the narrator and Homer shortly, but suffice it to say now that Homer is a "master" in the literary sense, in that his work is the source from which Walcott's derives. The term "master" also calls to mind the colonizer/colonized relationship and, in the process of Walcott's using the term, it is ironized: Homer, the "original" "master," must now rely on Walcott for his voice. With St. Lucia as his setting and through the interactions of characters lifted from the *Iliad*, characters of Walcott's own invention like Major Dennis Plunkett and his wife Maud, as well as a manifestation of Homer himself as "Omeros," Walcott builds a narrative that works as a meditation on a Caribbean writer's relationship to a European literary heritage. Through this process he is able to critique the drive for empire which has rested at the heart of European endeavors around the world.

In this way Walcott's thinking reflects much critical theory of the last few decades, especially the famous examination by Edward W. Said in *Orientalism* of the ways in which imperialism controls the perspectives cultures have of one another. Insofar as Orientalism is "a created body of theory and practice in which, for many generations, there has been considerable material investment," Said says it exists as "configurations of power" through which Europe can reinforce its vitality by comparing itself to a "weaker" Orient.[9] Said calls this "the formidable structure of cultural domination" and notes it is always invested with particular ideological ends in mind.[10] He continues his study of the effects of "cultural domination" in *Culture and Imperialism*. There he notes, "At some very basic level, imperialism means thinking about, settling on, controlling land that you do not possess, that is distant, that is lived on and owned by others."[11] In *Omeros* this impulse is represented by the characters of Maud and Major Plunkett who persist on the island despite the ending of Britain's active colonization of it. Also relevant to a study of Walcott's poem is Said's insight that "Partly because of empire, all cultures are involved in one another; none is single and pure, all are hybrid, heterogeneous, extraordinarily differentiated, and unmonolithic."[12] Indeed, one of the hallmarks of Walcott's poem is its desire to show how interwoven the history of St. Lucia is with European powers and the references to Homer help to illustrate this linkage.

The other quality of Walcott's work mentioned, its self-reflexivity, is addressed in that other ubiquitous "post" in current critical theory, apart from postcolonialism: postmodernism. Linda Hutcheon points out that postmodernism is typically seen as "politically ambivalent" whereas postcolonialism, by definition, contains a "strong political motivation."[13] She concludes that the two share a number of strategies: irony, allegory, and self-reflexivity.[14] They also share a preoccupation with marginalized figures whom she calls the "ex-centric" in another work.[15] Kwame Anthony Appiah similarly compares the terms "postcolonial" and "postmodern" and offers a useful view of the prefix shared by the two: "[T]he *post* in postcolonial, like the post in postmodern is the *post* of the space-clearing gesture" he explains.[16] He writes that it is a "post that challenges earlier legitimating narratives."[17] Thus Appiah does not feel historically constrained by the "post" in postcolonial as Ashcroft and the others believed was the inevitable effect of the prefix. Instead Appiah views it as a tool to distinguish the present from the past. Walcott's work is certainly "post" in the sense that *Omeros* can be read as a "space-clearing gesture" in which the legacy of Homer and Western literature can finally be engaged with the intent to move beyond them. Yet the problems of empire are still tangibly present in the poem, a "continuing process" as Ashcroft, Griffiths, and Tiffin argue.

The question is, how does postmodern self-reflexivity aid Walcott in his examination of Homer? This question gets to the heart of the effectiveness of self-reflexivity.[18] Is a literature which is so consumed with itself and its own mannerisms, as postmodernism is sometimes said to be, also capable of addressing social concerns? Can it still be a tool for political expression and indignation if it is also willfully self-obsessed? I would argue that self-reflexivity is operative in Walcott's poem to the extent that we cannot suspend our disbelief because we are constantly made aware of a narrator constructing the poem as it goes on. Through this self-reflexivity Walcott can both recognize his debt to Homer and acknowledge the Western cultural demands which are an obstacle for the poem's characters. The self-reflexivity works as a qualifying device, then, one which allows Walcott to remain cognizant of his own motives at the same time that he questions Homer's.

Finally, I would like to evoke the aspect of postcolonial studies that Gayatri Spivak famously examines in "Can the Subaltern Speak?" She asks if it is possible for the "subaltern," the oppressed colonial subject, to speak for him- or herself within the colonial situation. In the end she remains dubious of the possibility, particularly as these individuals are co-opted by critical theory; she asks, "How can we touch the consciousness of the people even as we investigate their politics?"[19] Looking at this issue from another point of view, Homi K. Bhabha calls our attention to the need to analyze the voices which emerge from imperial conditions. He argues,

> if the interest in postmodernism is limited to a celebration of the fragmentation of the "grand narratives" of postenlightenment rationalism then, for all its intellectual excitement, it remains a profoundly parochial enterprise.

> The wider significance of the postmodern condition lies in the awareness that the epistemological "limits" of those ethnocentric ideas are also enunciative boundaries of a range of other dissonant, even dissident histories and voices—women, the colonized, minority groups, the bearers of policed sexuality . . . It is in this sense that the boundary becomes the place from which *something begins its presencing.*[20]

Walcott speaks from a historically marginalized position, along "the boundary" as Bhabha's metaphor has it, within European thought. His project entails giving "ex-centric" individuals voice, as Hutcheon advocates and Bhabha here calls for. Indeed, part of the significance of Walcott's poem is its ability to dramatize postcolonial conflicts. The mutual identification which occurs between its characters by the end of the poem goes a long way toward showing how, once different groups have gained a voice, they can work to find common ground for understanding one another, presumably leading to an improvement in their shared postcolonial condition.

A number of studies on Walcott have thoroughly examined the Homeric parallels with *Omeros*, so it would be superfluous for me to do the same here.[21] While I will make a few references to Homer's text as I go on, my primary concern is with what we find in Walcott; after all, the poet claims in interviews never to have read the whole of Homer's poems.[22] It is thus the idea of Homer, as much as Homer himself, which Walcott reacts against.[23] I want to examine Walcott's relationship to the notion of the origin as it is manifested in the figure of Homer as well as in Achille's return to Africa. To do this I will first survey the intense self-reflexivity operative in the poem, particularly in regard to the ways in which it aids Walcott's narrator in engaging Homer. Then I will study how the notion of origin becomes conflated with naming in *Omeros* as the poem's protagonist, Achille, seeks to fabricate his own origin story. Finally I will reflect on the implications of calling *Omeros* an epic poem. My belief is that Walcott employs self-reflexivity to engage a notion of origins which he wishes to acknowledge but also transcend.

"Omeros" and Postmodern Self-Reflexivity

Before looking into self-reflexivity in *Omeros*, I want to consider its use with the themes of epic, empire, and origins in a poem from Walcott's *Selected Poems* of 1964. This volume contains a piece appropriately titled, for our purposes, "Origins." The poem begins with its speaker commenting, "I came among olives of algae,/Foetus of Plankton, I remember nothing."[24] In *Omeros*, the figure of Homer will also emerge from the sea. The name of the speaker of "Origins" goes unstated but nevertheless he begins a catalog of heroes from the classical epic and appears to address a Homer-like figure:[25] "I learnt your annals of ocean/Of Hector, bridler of horses,/Achilles, Aeneas, Ulysses" (*CP*, 11). The speaker thus positions himself as one responding to the epic tradition, but his lack of a specified identity (his "namelessness") does not permit us to situate him any further. After his invocation of epic heroes, the speaker of "Origins" offers an image with a strikingly textual basis: "Blank pages turn in the wind" (*CP*, 11). The metaphor utilized in this line ("blank pages") anticipates similar text-based images in *Omeros*. The pages are blank because they await a poet like Walcott to fill them—that is, for the marginalized to be present among the literary characters (Achilles, Aeneas, etc.) who represent the apex of Western classical heroism. In this way Walcott responds to the need identified by Bhabha to represent those whose story has yet to be written.

Walcott's desire to fill the "blank pages" of history becomes clearer in "Origins'" second section. The speaker comments, "Between the Greek and African pantheon,/Lost animist, I rechristened trees" (*CP*, 12). The speaker looks to an alternative tradition, an "animist" one which will help him diversify his worldview outside of a Greek frame of reference. Achille in *Omeros* will similarly attempt to reconnect with his own African origins. Although "Origins" is largely hermetic, its speaker is clearly trying to recover some lost origin and the second section ends with a reference to a "Guinean odyssey" (*CP*, 12). The speaker considers that which has been lost; he remarks, "I seek my own name and a man" (*CP*, 14) echoing Virgil's opening of the *Aeneid*: "I sing of arms and of a man."[26] In contrast with celebrated characters like Aeneas, the poem concludes by fulfilling its promise to draw attention to the underrepresented figures who do the work that goes uncelebrated:

> We praise those whose back on hillsides buckles on the wind
> To sow the grain of Guinea in the mouths of the dead,
> ....
> Who kneel in the open sarcophagi of cocoa
> To hallow the excrement of our martyrdom and fear,
> Whose sweat, touching earth, multiplies in crystals of sugar
> Those who conceive the birth of white cities in a raindrop
> And the annihilation of races in the prism of the dew. (*CP*, 15–16)

In "Origins" issues of race and social dominance are discussed in a framework which makes reference to the figures of the classical epic—a strategy Walcott will adopt on a grander scale in *Omeros*. The self-reflexivity early in the poem (the blank pages) proves a memorable metaphor for those figures whose history has yet to be written; it will be Walcott's job to do this in *Omeros*.

At nearly 330 pages, *Omeros* contains ample space for the development of the self-reflexive strategies that aid its examination of the postcolonial issues first raised in "Origins." The poem is notably most self-reflexive when describing the lives of the characters Walcott adds to those he draws directly from Homer, namely Major Plunkett and his wife. Early in the poem the narrator offers an aside that reveals the self-reflexive nature of his relationship to these characters: "This wound I have stitched into Plunkett's character./He has to be wounded, affliction is one theme/of this work, this fiction, since every 'I' is a // fiction finally. Phantom narrator, resume" (*O*, 28). The call for the "phantom narrator" to proceed after the interpolation of the authorial voice draws attention to the "metaliterary" nature of Walcott's work. The reader is forced, in other words, to pay close attention to the way the poem constructs itself; there is little chance for us to be swept away by what is otherwise a rather conventional narrative. The narrator's commentary qualifies the figure of Plunkett: if he seems an unfeeling colonizer—who dreams at one point of traveling over the expanse of the declining British empire (O, 90)—it is because he is a necessary "fiction," a figure who must be present to represent the colonial history of the island. The wound "stitched" into Plunkett's character—and here we might recall the Greek term "rhapsody," which means to "stitch together," as well as the fact that the Homeric singers were called rhapsodes[27]—provides balance to the wound carried by the native fisherman Philocte who plays a small part in Homer's poem but a larger one in the play by Sophocles *Philoctetes*. We learn of Philoctete's wound[28] within the first two pages of the poem when he shows tourists "a scar made by a rusted anchor . . . puckered like the corolla/of a sea-urchin" on his leg (O, 4). The wounds suggest how both the colonizer (Plunkett) and colonized (Philoctete) are afflicted by the history of empire. The figures Walcott appropriates from the *Iliad* (including Philoctetes) are largely free from the self-reflexive commentary which Walcott applies to Plunkett and Maud. Walcott foregrounds the additions he makes to the Homeric dramatis personae, thereby exhibiting reverence for Homer even as he adds to the ancient poet's cast of characters.

To suggest the end of the age of imperialism, Maud, who reluctantly stays on at St. Lucia despite yearnings for her native Ireland, dies near the end of the tale.[29] While Maud's death is one of the more touching moments in the narrative and is told in a sympathetic way by the narrator, it too is marked by a self-reflexivity which makes it difficult to read Maud as a "real" person instead of as a character intended for allegorical purposes. The narrator—that fictional "I"—notes when Maud dies, "I was attending/the funeral of a character I'd created;/the fiction of her life needed a good ending // as much as mine" (O, 266). The fate of the poem's speaker *is* tied up with Maud's insofar as her death signifies an historical shift for him as the remnants of empire slowly fade away. We might recall the line the speaker of the poem utters to Omeros: "Master, I was the freshest of all your readers." This declaration receives no real elaboration in the text, but presumably it is through his reinvention of Homer in a Caribbean setting that the narrator sees himself as able to read Homer in the "freshest" of ways. Maud's death similarly reflects the "freshness" of Walcott's reading: the aggression of the Greeks against the Trojans is not unlike the intrusion of the British into St. Lucia, and by bringing about Maud's demise Walcott suggests this period of forced influence has reached its terminus.

The figure of Omeros in the poem, the "master" in both the literary and the colonial senses, offers an extended case study in self-reflexivity. He fails to appear fully until relatively late, at which time it is the narrator's task to update the ancient poet on the changes that have occurred since his passing so many centuries ago. Despite his late appearance, he is anticipated early on, in the following passage from the poem's second chapter: "*O* was the conch-shell's invocation, *mer* was/both mother and sea in our Antillean patois,/*os*, a grey bone, and the white surf as it crashes // and spreads its sibilant collar on a lace shore" (*O*, 14. Walcott's emphasis). The emphasis on the morphemes that make up Omeros's name ("O," "mer," "os") suggests he is composed entirely of text; here again, like Maud and Plunkett, Omeros is more a literary device than a dynamic character. When Omeros finally does appear, he rises from the sea, which the metaphor in Walcott's "invocation" foreshadows. This is only one of many references to the sea, another of which I will study in a moment. These references recall not only the geographical boundaries of St. Lucia but they also suggest the timelessness of the ways of life on the island that reflect themes which first appear in Homer. One of these themes is the sea voyage as a metaphor for the course of life. The voyage will figure prominently in Achille's search for origins.

The poem is fashioned out of terza rima-like stanzas which are undoubtedly intended to draw to mind the *Divine Comedy*. Invoking Dante's canonical poem adds yet another difficulty to the already complex task of deciding how *Omeros* relates to the generic expectations of the epic. We are aided in this task, however, by the interaction between Omeros and the narrator. Near the poem's end Omeros plays Virgil to the narrator's Dante: the narrator must undertake a journey to an underworld, an Inferno of sorts, which is inhabited by past poets. Here he is forced to confront the demands of his vocation. Omeros explains,

> Your wanderer is a phantom from the boy's shore.
>
> Mark you, *he* does not go; he sends his narrator;
> he plays tricks with time because there are two journeys
> in every odyssey, one on worried water,
>
> the other crouched and motionless, without noise.
> For both, the "I" is a mast; a desk is a raft
> for one, foaming with paper, and dipping the beak
>
> of a pen in its foam. (*O*, 291. Walcott's emphasis)

The problematic nature of the "I" in narrative poetry, reiterated here again, was also emphasized in the passage on Plunkett's wound reviewed earlier. The metaphor is telling: the "I" and his narration are compared to a sea craft, drawing to mind the voyage of Odysseus. There is another ramification of the metaphor as well: if the labyrinthine voyage of Odysseus is taken as an emblem for the circuits in life one must travel to reach enlightenment, it is also indicative of the tangled process of writing, especially when one attempts to engage one's literary progenitor as directly as Walcott seeks to do in this poem. The "I" is both a metaphor for the impulse that drives the narration (as the mast on which the sail is hung) as well as visually evocative of the mast itself. In this way the "I" goes from being a signifier to something close to a signified. Walcott's recognition of the arbitrariness of the sign enables him to question his own enterprise. If language involves the kind

Chapter Three

of connotative and denotative slipperiness suggested here, how can he use it to adequately represent his narrator's relationship to the past, especially to a literary juggernaut like Homer?

The answer to this question lies with the poem's self-reflexivity. The self-awareness it confers on the poem helps to keep *Omeros* from naively interpreting its relationship to the past. For instance, when one considers the genre to which the poem is typically assigned—the epic—*Omeros's* self-reflexive nature is all the more important. I will return to the implications that come with calling *Omeros* an epic at the end of this chapter. Suffice it to say now, however, that the poem uses self-reflexivity to question its epic leanings:

> The ocean had
>
> no memory of the wanderings of Gilgamesh,
> or whose sword severed whose head in the *Iliad*.
> It was an epic where every line was erased
>
> yet freshly written with sheets of exploding surf
> ....
> . . . it drenched every survivor
>
> with blessing. It never altered its metre
> to suit the age, a wide page without metaphors.
> Our last resort as much as yours, Omeros. (*O*, 295–96)

This passage calls on the reader to remember the sea imagery employed earlier in the text, in the references to Homer's name as well as in the image of the speaker's desk as a raft. Like the ocean, which has no concern for the changing styles or conventions of human society ("it never altered its metre"), the conflicts of Walcott's poem work to show how the history of cultural aggression, which is a condition not only of empire but apparently also of human nature (if the *Iliad* is taken as an example), stretches back to Homer's time and perhaps beyond. Walcott's self-reflexivity might be a factor of his postmodern condition but it ultimately allows him to be more mindful of his place in the continuum of world literature and stress how the postcolonial circumstances St. Lucia finds itself in are symptomatic of the history of the West from Homer's age forward.

If self-reflexivity is taken as a premier strategy of postmodern writers, as Linda Hutcheon proposes, we can begin to see, judging from Walcott's example, the ways in which it can help to qualify a writer's perspective on origins. While self-reflexivity (like postmodernism in Hutcheon's view) is "politically ambivalent" in and of itself, it clearly can be used to political ends. The precedent found in "Origins," which uses postmodern self-reflexivity to draw attention to the marginalization of particular groups of people, is carried through in *Omeros*. Walcott answers Bhabha's call for postmodernism to go beyond only disrupting "the 'grand narratives' of postenlightenment rationalism" by speaking for those who have been historically underrepresented. I will now focus on two of the main characters of *Omeros*—Helen and Achille—to illustrate how Walcott uses a direct critique of origins to complement his work with self-reflexivity. My central question is if Walcott is successful in disrupting the "grand narrative" of narration itself, of calling into question the stability of the literary text by pointing to the instability of language from which it is built, can his poem also address the social problems of the island in a manner which sheds further light on its relationship to the rest of the world?

Helen, Achille's Search for Origins, and the Politics of Naming

We have seen how concepts like "history" and "empire" are important in *Omeros* and indeed the terms themselves are repeated throughout the text.[30] With the consistent repetition of these words Walcott conditions our reading of the poem: their reiteration ensures that the reader will stay attuned to them, even as he or she attempts to follow the unfolding plot. The terms work together, then, to aid the reader in understanding the degree to which the

Chapter Three

legacy of Homer, as a representative of the West, as an image of what Said calls "cultural domination," is an obstacle for the narrator. The narrator asks, "[W]hen would it stop/the echo in the throat, insisting, 'Omeros';/when would I enter that light beyond metaphor" (O, 271). In some sense the poet is confined by his own "metaphor": if Homer is conceived as the origin from which Walcott's narrator descends, this direct address to the classical poet can be regarded as a way of contending with his historical legacy. On the other hand, the poet is also indebted to Homer because his poem would not exist otherwise, depending as it does on its appropriation and recasting of Homer's characters.

We might recall that the action of Homer's *Iliad* begins with a conflict between Achilles, the Greeks' greatest fighter, and King Agamemnon. Agamemnon is told by the gods to return the stolen daughter of a Trojan he has taken and out of resentment he demands Achilles' prize for his own. This leads to Achilles' "rage"—the very first word in the poem and a term that is repeated consistently over the duration of the story,[31] like Walcott's use of "history" and "empire"—and his abandonment of his fellow Greek warriors.[32] By contrast, the conflict in *Omeros* centers on the desire for Helen shared by Achille and his rival Hector. This Achille, however, differs considerably from his Homeric namesake: Walcott's Achille is a rather ineffectual main character who only takes action when he embarks on a quest for his origins. I have already noted how two characters of Walcott's own invention, Major Plunkett and his wife Maud, are representatives of colonizing forces in the poem. They employ Helen as a housekeeper—one way for Walcott to illustrate the subservient economic position natives of the island are forced to assume as a result of colonization. Another local figure, Ma Kilman, extends Walcott's analogy between the characters of St. Lucia and those of Homer by assuming the role of an oracle of sorts; she is called a "sybil," and eventually cures Philocte of his festering leg wound (O, 58). This healing occurs at the end of the poem and suggests an easing of the wounds caused by imperialism. It asks us to read *Omeros* as an optimistic poem, as a chronicle of the passing away of a dark period of history for the island.

Helen is at the center of *Omeros*, as she is in Homer's poem. Early in the story, the narrator comments, "Plunkett, in his innocence, // had tried to change History to a metaphor,/in the name of a housemaid; I, in self-defence,/altered her opposite. Yet it was all for her" (*O*, 270). This statement works as a summation of the respective problems of both Plunkett, the imperialist, and the narrator, the island native. The two characters focus their relationship to history through Helen. For Plunkett she is both an object of desire and pity. For the narrator she is emblematic of the compromised status of the islanders. The subordinate position forced on Helen is evident in the poem, not only in her role as a maid to the Plunketts, but also in a scene in which she arrives at the Plunketts' house to borrow money. Ultimately she turns away from the money she asks for in defiance. In this gesture Helen indicates she has become cognizant of her subservient status and has repudiated it. The narrator concludes, "There, in her head of ebony,/there was no real need for the historian's/remorse, nor for literature's. Why not see Helen // as the sun saw her, with no Homeric shadow[?]" (*O*, 271). Like her refusal of the money, the narrator wants Helen to make a break with her past image, to move beyond the "Homeric shadow" which shrouds her, in his view and in ours.

The drawback to Walcott's literary appropriation of Homer's Helen is that it is difficult for the reader to see her without her "Homeric shadow" if only because her name cannot fail to call to mind the famous Helen of Walcott's source text. However, in an attempt to illustrate the difference between the two versions of Helen—Homer's and his own—*Omeros*'s narrator supplies a useful comparison:

> These Helens are different creatures,
>
> one marble, one ebony. One unknots a belt
> of yellow cotton slowly from her shelving waist,
> one a cord of purple wool, the other one takes

Chapter Three

> a bracelet of white cowries from a narrow wrist;
> one lies in a room with olive-eyed mosaics,
> another in a beach shack with its straw mattress,
>
> but each draws an elbow slowly over her face
> and offers the gift of her sculptured nakedness,
> parting her mouth. (O, 313)

This gesture of Helen "parting her mouth," strikes the reader as peculiar. Surely, one would think Helen would be represented in a manner beyond the sexuality by which she has been defined for millennia in European literature. Helen appears still to carry the burden of the male gaze, an object of desire whether "marble" or "ebony." Yet the dark skin and impoverished conditions of *Omeros's* Helen forces the reader to reflect on the disparity between the material conditions of the narrator's native island (a "beach shack" with a "straw mat") and the riches of Western empires (a "room of olive-eyed mosaics"). The revealing contrast between the two Helens shows us precisely why Homer's poetics cannot be fully reflective of the narrator's experiences and why the *Iliad* must be made the subject of Walcott's revisionism. The narrator finds he must utilize materials from his own realm of reference, even as he appropriates characters or themes from Homer's tale.

As a way to combat the "Homeric shadow," the European influence, that casts itself over the island, Achille embarks on a search for his origins. Achille thus attempts to move beyond the Western inheritance which is also an obstacle for the poem's narrator. Achille's origin-seeking comes as a dream journey in which he returns to Africa to recover his ancestral heritage. In his dream Achille travels by boat, clearly paralleling the wanderings of Odysseus (and one might also recall the metaphor of the narrator's desk as a raft). Despite this promising return to his African source, which had up to this time been unavailable to him, Achille fails to escape the watchful eye of the Christian god of the imperialist. His journey is given official sanction by this god whose very presence prevents Achille from remembering the names of the African deities with whom he feels he must reconnect:

> Now the strange, inimical river surrenders its stealth
> to the sunlight. And a light inside him wakes,
> skipping centuries, ocean and river, and Time itself.
>
> And God said to Achille, "Look, I giving you permission
> to come home. Is I send the sea-swift as a pilot,
> the swift whose wings is the sign of my crucifixion.
>
> And thou shalt have no God should in case you forgot
> my commandments." And Achille felt the homesick shame
> and pain of his Africa. His heart and his bare head
>
> were bursting as he tried to remember the name
> of the river- and the tree-god in which he steered,
> whose hollow body carried him to the settlement ahead.
> (O, 134)

The importance of names in this section of the poem ("he tried to remember the name") will recur when Achille speaks with Afolabe, his father; it is precisely this remembrance of the old names which the "albino god" disallows (O, 139). The transformation of God's language into a dialect familiar to Achille ("Is I send," etc.) suggests that God dominates the actions of Achille, even as He is rendered in Achille's own image.[33] The figure of Homer in the poem similarly speaks in Achille's dialect late in the narrative (O, 317). Paula Burnett points out, "[I]t is entirely logical that an individual's interior dialogue with his God would make use of his own language."[34] But this is not Achille's god by choice; it is a god who imposes himself on Achille. There is the sense here, then, that the relationship of Achille to God parallels Walcott's own relationship to Homer which similarly oscillates between dutiful reverence and subversion. Much as Achille must contend with the Christian god, so too must Walcott wrestle with the legacy of Homer.

Achille's voyage eventually carries him to Africa, where he meets with his long lost father, Afolabe. The dialogue between the two characters proves the poem's most important meditation on naming and the effectiveness of its medium—language—in reflecting perceptions of reality. Afolabe asks his son, "Achille. What does the name mean? I have forgotten the one that I gave you." Achille responds:

> Well, I too have forgotten.
>
> Everything was forgotten. You also. I do not know.
> The deaf sea has changed around every name that you gave
> us; trees, men, we yearn for a sound that is missing. (O, 137)

It is significant that the idiom Achille uses here, a more grammatically "correct" register of English, appears nowhere else in his speech in the poem. Only in his dream vision, when he is closest to his unconscious mind, can he express his desire to connect with the origins of his culture, to recover those lost names, that "sound that is missing" which could offer some clue as to his source. He hopes to do this in a way less bound by the particulars of his perspective, as represented by his dialect. Achille's use of "standard" English stands in contrast to the "sub-standard" English utilized in God's exhortation to him. God is more constrained than Achilles because he is nothing more than a disembodied discourse echoing in Achille's head; Achille, by contrast, is a character with substance beyond his distinctive speaking style.

Afolabe answers Achille's inquiry into names by noting,

> A name means something. The qualities desired in a son
> ....
> . . . since every name is a blessing,
> since I am remembering the hope I had for you as a child.

> Unless the sound means nothing. Then you would be
> nothing.
> Did they think you were nothing in that other kingdom? (O, 137)

Clearly Afolabe believes in the importance of naming that Achille intimated when struggling with the Christian god. But Achille expresses ambivalence: "I do not know what the name means. It means something/maybe. What's the difference?" he asks (O, 138). Afolabe answers him: "[I]f you're content with not knowing what our names mean, // then I am not Afolabe, your father . . . you, nameless son, are only the ghost // of a name" (O, 138–39). Afolabe's words are intended to teach his son the importance of remembering the names and thus remembering the past. Yet Afolabe also places an emphasis on the signifier which will prove unhelpful to Achille. At the end of the poem, when many of the other characters appear to have attained some degree of self-awareness, Achille is still stricken with a preoccupation with origins that does him little good. His anxiety with origin-finding might be traced to Afolabe's suggestion that Achille could become a function of the signifier, a "ghost of a name," if he does not recognize the importance of naming. Significantly, Achille's name shifts in the last pages of the poem from "Achille" to "Achilles" (O, 324). The instability of the signifier used to represent Achille himself suggests the narrator's distrust of Achille's preoccupation with names and the instability of Achille's identity. It also hints at a momentary conflation of Homer's Achilles and Walcott's Achille. Although unlike in most ways, they share a stubbornness that consistently disregards the desires and perspectives of others. They merge, if only for this brief moment, as Walcott's Achille attains the same level of self-absorption as his Homeric precursor.

Just as *Omeros*'s interest in self-reflexivity and the epic are anticipated in "Origins," so too is its concern with naming presaged by a short poem entitled "Names" from Walcott's volume *Sea Grapes* (1976). Here Walcott offers a vision of an unnamed people, again compared metaphorically with the sea: "My race began as the sea began,/with no nouns, and with no horizon" (*CP*, 305). This "race" is given names, given a "horizon" and a boundary, by others. Subjectivity appears to be an unwelcome gift to these people: "[M]y race began like the osprey/with that cry,/that terrible vowel,/that I!" (*CP*, 306). As an act of subversion these names are disregarded by the people to whom they are attached: "with nothing in our hands // but this stick/to trace our names on the sand/which the sea erased again, to our indifference" (*CP*, 306). Bhabha has written of this poem, "[I]t signifies the destiny of culture as a site, not simply of subversion and transgression, but one that prefigures a kind of solidarity between ethnicities that meet in the tryst of colonial history."[35] Indeed, Walcott's interest in nomination is tied in with his study of the power of language when used as a political tool. We saw this first with God's words to Achille and then again in the exchange between Achille and Afolabe. In both cases language and naming are means for expressing the characters' relationship with origins.

There is a distinction to be made here, between "imposed" origins, as Homer is to Walcott and the Christian god is to Achille, and what we might call "elected" origins as Achille attempts to construct with his return to Africa. Despite the different sources of these origins—whether they come from one's self or from others—the outcome turns out to be much the same. Achille can establish his own origin story and thereby repudiate the Christian god, but he is ultimately no more empowered when he does so. This is apparent in the final appearance of the theme of naming in *Omeros*, near the poem's end. After being reunited with Helen after the death of Hector, Achille suggests that they give Helen's unborn child an African name. Ma Kilman tells us, "'Helen/don't want no African child./[Achille] say he'll leave it // till the day of the christening. That Helen must learn/where she from'" (*O*, 318). Helen is unmoved by Achille's argument and rejects his proposal; she thus also rejects the origin Achille wishes to evoke. Helen embodies the narrator's argument that there is little to be gained by a return to the origin, whether it is of one's own choosing or not. If Helen agreed with Achille she would be replacing one origin with another. Neither origin offers her a way to move beyond the problems of the past; in fact they both keep her resolutely centered in the past. Hope for the island rests in some middle ground between acknowledging its history but also looking toward its future.

It is perhaps in this way that the poem's admission that "all colonies inherit their empire's sin" makes sense (O, 208). Helen's indifference to an African past is a consequence of her subjection to British rule. On the other hand, Walcott also suggests the future of the island does not rest with a return to some origin. Ultimately it is within the powers of the inhabitants of the island itself, and not outsiders, to affect the changes that bring closure to the poem: Ma Kilman heals the wound of Philoctete, a wound that can be seen as a metaphor for the afflictions of history and empire; Omeros comes to stay on at St. Lucia not as a European but as a transformed figure who enthusiastically acclimates himself to island life and assumes a speech style akin to Achille's; racial divisions are at least partially transcended as Major Plunkett's affinities with Helen are confirmed in a "moment [that] bound him for good to another race" (O, 307). Differences remain, of course: there are still separate "races." But Plunkett has come to value his status as an islander over his place in the once-British Empire. The origin for these various characters has been effaced: Plunkett leaves behind his British identity much as Achille is forced to dispense with his African identity by Helen's refusal of his proposal. Origins, whether they are a product of one's birthright (Plunkett), or a matter of one's own selection (Achille), are questioned at the end of the poem.

"Omeros" as an Epic?

Despite Philoctete's healing, some wounds stand witness to the effects of history and empire. The poem's narrator, after his meeting with Plunkett, remarks on "the wound of a language I'd no wish to remove" (O, 270). The "language" which is a "wound" is of course English, the idiom that mediates his relationship to Homer. Language can indeed be an affliction, as we saw in Achille's rela-

Chapter Three

tionship to God as well as in Afolabe's threat that Achille could become a "ghost of a name." Yet language also permits the wounds of history to be remembered in *Omeros* by the process of recounting them within the narration. This does not imply, however, that history should be taken at face value. In his Nobel Prize address, "The Antilles: Fragments of Epic Memory," Walcott argues,

> For every poet it is always morning in the world. History a forgotten, insomniac night; History and elemental awe are always our early beginning, because the fate of poetry is to fall in love with the world, in spite of History.[36]

This curious mixture of an awareness of the past but also a willingness to move beyond its tragedies informs many of Walcott's writings, *Omeros* preeminent among them. Although early in the poem Plunkett can wonder at "how time could be reworded,/ which is the historian's task" in an attempt to render history in his own image, by the end his historiographic impulses have ebbed away as he comes to feel a real connection with his fellow islanders (*O*, 95). The island's conflicts have not been entirely resolved at the close of the poem, despite the symbolic and literal healing of Philoctete's wound, but there is the sense that a new epoch of greater respect and dignity is dawning. This is a moment in which the inhabitants of the island, from Plunkett to Achille, can be united in their love of the island. It is thus "always morning in the world," always a new origin that renders the past origin obsolete.

The poem confirms this notion of moving forward with its ending. Instead of echoing Homer, its last chapter closes with an outright inversion of him. In place of Achille's "rage," the narrator of Walcott's poem declares, "I sang of quiet Achille" (*O*, 320). "Quiet" is an apt term: throughout the poem Achille is essentially an ineffectual individual, to whom Helen returns only after her loss of Hector. When he does assert himself, in suggesting they give Helen's baby an African name, he is immediately rebuffed. Achille stands as an illustration of the way history and empire have weighed on the islanders; his diffidence mirrors his compromised position. This leads me back to the question of *Omeros's* status as an epic. If Achille is to be seen as an epic hero, he is an odd one indeed. His over-valuing of the importance of naming represents a position which clearly offers little opportunity for advancement. Achille seems more an anti-hero, not only in the sense that he is the antithesis to Homer's character of the same name who is filled with passionate "rage" at the beginning of the *Iliad*, but also because he fails to acquire the self-awareness which appears to have come to many characters of the poem like Helen and Plunkett.

The audience of *Omeros* is intended as Caribbean;[37] the narrator remarks, "I sang our wide country, the Caribbean Sea" (*O*, 320). This declaration lends support to the contention that Walcott is working within the confines of the epic tradition in that he adopts a public voice intended for didactic purposes. However, the inversion of Homeric themes and ideals, like the hero, undermines the poem as epic in any conventional sense. I suggest Walcott should be regarded as using elements of the epic to produce a poem which is of its age politically and stylistically—it is "hybrid" in the sense Terry Eagleton uses the term to characterize postmodern art.[38] When he is asked if *Omeros* is "the great Caribbean epic," Walcott responds,

> I think it would be a terrible irony for the Caribbean, if just for the sake of dignifying a race, of saying: this poem is going to redeem history . . . It would be a terrible kind of presumption—I think. So, I certainly didn't want to do that. All I wanted to do was to celebrate the diurnal, day-to-day heroism of people who go out and face the arrogance. Is that destiny? Well, yes, that's admirable. Because such people—fishermen—the ordinary lives that are depicted—they have no idea of expanding power. They think they relate to power—they relate to the power of the weather and the power that has been in their past—in history and slavery, and so on.
> And that's why I resist so much the idea of this poem as being epic in its undertaking. It has elements of epic. It has widths. It has a variety of subjects, and—I suppose—you can say it has

Chapter Three

> heroes, in a way. But there is not a sort of label outside that says: I will now undertake . . . to justify, or condemn, or redeem history.[39]

Walcott points to the political dimensions of the term "epic" here, and in his admission that he has no interest in "redeem[ing] history" he indicates that the poem is intended to stand witness to history. In this process the poem must acknowledge its origins even as it calls them into question with its self-reflexivity.[40] To the extent that Walcott attempts to break away from Eurocentric thinking, we do his project a disservice when we hold it to European standards such as the epic.[41] We might say that the author's relation to the epic is similar to the island natives' relationship to the British: it is a "configuration of power," to use Said's phrase, which must be usurped to move beyond the master/servant binary colonization forces upon them.

Walcott's poem contains features of the epic, such as its use of a public voice and wide audience, its breadth and episodic narrative. But its employment of postmodern strategies like self-reflexivity and its inversion of the epic hero, Achille, suggest a movement beyond the strictures of the classical epic. There are problems with calling *Omeros* a "long poem" insofar as the long poem is a largely American form stemming from Whitman, as Thomas Gardner has shown, and in this sense it is a product of a different imperialist power.[42] Yet if we recognize the long poem's lack of genre conventions, we see it is pliable in a way not possible in the epic—or the lyric for that matter. The eclectic nature or Walcott's poem—its use of a verse form reminiscent of Dante, its appropriation of Homeric themes and characters, its densely-packed narrative style—calls to mind other postmodernist texts, such as Kenneth Koch's *Seasons on Earth* (1987) and Thomas McGrath's *Letter to an Imaginary Friend* (1997) which similarly employ elements of the epic to subversive ends. Projects like Walcott's help to expand the boundaries of the relatively recent tradition of the long poem to include those who have been historically voice-less; after all, this is what the long poem's early practitioner Whitman wished to do in his "celebration" of women and the culturally disenfranchised. Thus although Walcott's text is unique in many regards, the affinities it shares with many other poems written in the second half of the twentieth century help place it within the context of the postmodern long poem which embraces plurality and alternative points of view at the same time it foregrounds its own form and artifice through strategies like self-reflexivity. In the next chapter we will see how a poet based at the center of the English empire, Geoffrey Hill, similarly questions the hegemonic tendencies of European cultures while also foregrounding the formal elements of his text, including its language and use of anachronism.

Endnotes

1. Luigi Sampietro, *Derek Walcott on "Omeros": An Interview*, <http://users.unimi.it/ caribana/OnOmeros.html>.
2. It is worth noting, as evidence of Walcott's status as a recognized postcolonial thinker, that Ashcroft, Griffiths, and Tiffin include his prose piece "The Muse of History" in their *Post-Colonial Studies Reader*.
3. Bill Ashcroft, Gareth Griffiths, and Helen Tiffin, eds., *The Post-Colonial Studies Reader* (New York: Routledge, 1995), 2.
4. Ashcroft, et al, *Post-Colonial Studies*, 2.
5. John Thieme, *Derek Walcott* (New York: Manchester University Press, 1999), 2.
6. Homer's epics themselves are usually understood to have been the products of ages of retellings and elaborations by generations of poets and thus stood at a distance from their own "origin," although they may have been "corrected" by subsequent literate editors. See Gregory Nagy's *Poetry as Performance: Homer and Beyond* (New York: Cambridge University Press, 1996) for a recent evaluation of the classical epic in performance.
7. Simone Weil, *"The Iliad"; or the Poem of Force: A Critical Edition*, trans. and ed. James P. Holoka (New York: Peter Lang, 2003), 45.
8. Derek Walcott, *Omeros* (New York: Noonday, 1990), 283. Hereafter cited in the text as O.

Chapter Three

9 Edward Said, *Orientalism* (New York: Vintage, 1978), 5; 6.
10 Said, *Orientalism*, 25.
11 Edward Said, *Culture and Imperialism* (New York: Vintage, 1993), 7.
12 Said, *Culture*, xxv.
13 Linda Hutcheon, "Circling the Downspout of Empire," in *The Post-Colonial Studies Reader*, ed. Ashcroft, Bill, Gareth Griffiths, and Helen Tiffin (New York: Routledge, 1995), 130.
14 Hutcheon, "Circling the Downspout," 135.
15 Linda Hutcheon, *A Poetics of Postmodernism: History, Theory, Fiction* (New York: Routledge, 1988), 65.
16 Kwame Anthony Appiah, "The Postcolonial and the Postmodern," in *The Post-Colonial Studies Reader*, ed. Ashcroft, Bill, Gareth Griffiths, and Helen Tiffin (New York: Routledge, 1995), 119. Appiah's emphasis.
17 Appiah, "Postcolonial," 123.
18 In Terry Eagleton's view, postmodernism's self-reflexivity is one aspect of its general "depthlessness": "The typical postmodernist work of art is arbitrary, eclectic, hybrid, decentered, fluid, discontinuous, pastiche-like. True to the tenets of postmodernity, it spurns metaphysical profundity for a kind of contrived depthlessness, playfulness and lack of affect, an art of pleasures, surfaces and passing intensities . . . Rejecting all attempts to reflect a stable reality beyond itself, it exists self-consciously at the level of form or language" (*Literary Theory: An Introduction*, 2nd ed. [Minneapolis: University of Minnesota Press, 1996], 201). Fredric Jameson similarly posits the possibility that "Postmodernism, postmodern consciousness, may then amount to not much more than theorizing its own condition of possibility" (*Postmodernism; or, The Cultural Logic of Late Capitalism* [Durham: Duke University Press, 1991], ix).
19 Gayatri Chakravorty Spivak, "Can the Subaltern Speak," in *The Post-Colonial Studies Reader*, ed. Bill Ashcroft, Gareth Griffiths, and Helen Tiffin (New York: Routledge, 1995), 27.
20 Homi K. Bhabha, *The Location of Culture* (New York: Routledge, 1994), 4–5. Bhabha's emphasis.
21 As might be expected, Walcott's poem has received a fair amount

of critical attention, particularly in regard to its status as a modern epic, or revision of the epic tradition. One of Walcott's most prolific critics, Robert D. Hamner, calls *Omeros* an "epic of the dispossessed" because of its utilization of characters representing those who have been historically marginalized (*Epic of the Dispossessed: Derek Walcott's "Omeros"* [Columbia: University of Missouri Press, 1997]). Lorna Hardwick analyzes the use of simile in Homer and Walcott and concludes it operates as a means for Walcott to engage his Homeric forbearer ("Reception as Simile: The Poetics of Reversal in Homer and Derek Walcott," *International Journal of the Classical Tradition* 3.3 [Winter 1997]. Ebscohost. 3 March 2006. <http://web.ebscohost.com>). Charlotte S. McClure examines the image of Helen in Omeros and determines that Helen reveals the tension between Homeric mimicry and originality in the poem—Helen is an expression, in other words, of Walcott's debt to Homer as well as his desire to break away into "originality" ("'Helen of the 'West Indies': History or Poetry of a Caribbean Realm," *Studies in the Literary Imagination* 26 [Fall 1993]. Ebscohost. 3 March 2006. <http://web.ebscohost.com>). Charles Lock also looks at the figure of Helen and comments on her relative silence, surprising in a contemporary poem. He decides, however, that the silence of Helen is indicative of Walcott's own place within the politics of literary marginalization ("Derek Walcott's *Omeros*: Echoes from a White-Throated Vase." *Massachusetts Review* 40.1 [Spring 2000]. Ebscohost. 7 March 2006. <http://web.ebscohost.com>).

22 In his interview with Luigi Sampietro, Walcott comments, "I don't know the history of Achilles' activity in the *Iliad*. Maybe I was scared of the *Iliad* because—I don't *want* to be swallowed up, in a *sense*, by Homeric comparison." Walcott reveals a Bloomean "anxiety of influence" here which helps explain his continual denial of any intimate knowledge of Homer. In the same interview he says, "anybody looking through my references—my associations—they're simple associations that everybody knows: Odysseus, the Eternal Wanderer; or Helen, the Eternal Beauty; *or*, in this case, Achilles, the Eternal Warrior; or Hector . . . These are just magnified, very

ordinary symbols . . . Household names, really" (*Derek Walcott on "Omeros": An Interview*, <http://users.unimi.it/caribana/OnOmeros.html>. Walcott's emphasis).

23 Walcott makes reference to the series of "The World's Great Classics" at the end of Book I of his poem and thus alludes to the cultural capital assigned to particular texts as a result of their distribution as "canonical" works, as Homer represents (*O*, 71).

24 Derek Walcott, *Collected Poems: 1948–1984* (New York: Farrar, Straus and Giroux, 1986), 11. Hereafter cited in the text as *CP*.

25 He says he is "nameless" (*CP*, 11). This anonymity suggests that his is a general, "public" voice. The advantage of this anonymity is that he can speak for a wide group of people without his own motives for doing so becoming apparent. The disadvantage to this approach, of course, is that we do not know from where the speaker speaks. By contrast, the narrator's position in *Omeros* is quite evident and the poem works to foreground the point of view of this narrator. The issue of naming is also apparent in *Omeros*, as we shall see.

26 Virgil, *The Aeneid*, trans. Allen Mandelbaum (New York: Bantam, 1971), 1.

27 See Gregory Nagy's discussion of these figures in *Poetry as Performance*, particularly chapter 3.

28 Jahan Ramazani has analyzed the significance of the figure of Philoctete and his wound. He writes, "As graphic emblem of convulsive, bodily pain, the wound in *Omeros* memorializes the untold suffering of Afro-Caribbeans, yet as trope it inevitably poeticizes pain, compares this particular experience with others, and thus must either mar or deconstruct experiential uniqueness by plunging it into the whirlpool of metaphorical resemblance and difference" (*The Hybrid Muse: Postcolonial Poetry in English* [Chicago: University of Chicago Press, 2001], 71).

29 The name of this character calls to mind Tennyson's poem (*Maud: A Monodrama* [1855]) that tells the story of a narrator who loses his sanity over love for a woman called Maud. Maud's name also calls to mind W. B. Yeats's Maud Gonne who Yeats memorably likens to a second Helen.

30 The reevaluation of history occurs in other post-war book-length poems, perhaps most obviously in Robert Lowell's *History* (1973) and in Galway Kinnell's *The Book of Nightmares* (1971).
31 I hope not to imply here, however, that the concept of rage is monolithic in Homer's poem; as one blind reviewer of the present book pointed out, in Homer's poem there is a distinction between human rage and divine rage which clearly differ in character.
32 Homer, *The Iliad*, trans. Robert Fagles (New York: Penguin, 1990), 77.
33 This use of colloquial language in Walcott's poem is also in opposition to the classical epic and its use of a formalized diction. Bernard Knox offers a useful summary of epic poetics in his introduction to Robert Fagles' translation of Homer's epics. He notes, "[T]he language of Homer was one nobody, except epic bards, oracular priests or literary parodists would dream of using" (Bernard Knox, Introduction. *The Iliad* By Homer, trans. Robert Fagles [New York: Penguin, 1990], 11). This is not to say, however, that there are no colloquial elements to the speech of Homer's epics.
34 Paula Burnett, *Derek Walcott: Politics and Poetics* (Gainesville: University of Florida Press, 2000), 142.
35 Bhabha, *Location of Culture*, 231.
36 Derek Walcott, *What the Twilight Says* (New York: Farrar, Straus and Giroux, 1998), 79.
37 For an overview of the issue of Walcott's "literary" nature and how this separates him from Caribbean readers see Hamner's discussion in "Introduction to *Critical Perspectives on Derek Walcott*," *Three Dynamite Writers: Derek Walcott, Naguib Mahfouz, Wole Soyinka*, ed. Donald E. Herdeck (Colorado Springs: Three Continents Press, 1995), 9–12. Walcott's address of *Omeros* to Caribbean readers might be construed as an attempt to engage this audience whom he has been consistently accused of forgetting.
38 Eagleton, *Literary Theory: An Introduction*, 201.
39 Sampietro, *Derek Walcott on "Omeros": An Interview*, <http://users.unimi.it/caribana/OnOmeros.html>.
40 Self-reflexivity, as Linda Hutcheon has said, recurs throughout postmodern texts and indeed we might cite a number of postmodern

long poems, such as those by Armand Schwerner (*The Tablets*, 1999), James Merrill (*The Changing Light at Sandover*, 1982), John Berryman (*The Dream Songs*, 1969), Edward Dorn (*Gunslinger*, 1975), and many members of the "Language" School of poets (most importantly Charles Bernstein and Susan Howe), which use this device.

41 Even a critic as sensitive to Walcott's postcolonial position as Jahan Ramazani insists on calling *Omeros* a "Caribbean epic" (*The Hybrid Muse*, 49). I believe the liabilities of doing so far outweigh the advantages.

42 Thomas Gardner, *Discovering Ourselves in Whitman: The Contemporary American Long Poem* (Urbana: University of Illinois Press, 1989).

4

Narrating the Origins of the Nation: Geoffrey Hill's *Mercian Hymns* and "An Apology for the Revival of Christian Architecture in England"

Geoffrey Hill, the Nation, and Anglo-Saxonism

In chapter 1, I surveyed a number of writers who are inspired by Anglo-Saxon literature and culture. I showed that Pound argues "The Seafarer" (which he translated in 1911) and *Beowulf* are examples of an "indigenous art," "an art not newly borrowed."[1] Pound thus suggests there is something essentially "English" about this literature, thereby explaining why he would translate a line in his

Chapter Four

"Seafarer" as "'mid the English" when it is usually construed as "among the angels." Other figures preoccupied with Anglo-Saxon poetics, figures more on the periphery of modernism, include Basil Bunting (*Briggflatts*, 1966) and the Welsh poet and artist David Jones (*The Anathemata*, 1952) both of whom posit Anglo-Saxon England as an origin. Nicholas Howe points to Thom Gunn and the American Richard Wilbur as writers who represent the "afterlife" of Old English poetry.[2] Translations among leading poets in the last century are many, including Scottish poet Edwin Morgan's *Beowulf* (1952) and his version of the Anglo-Saxon "lyrics" in *Dies Irae* (1952). Seamus Heaney's *Beowulf* (2000) continues this tradition. Although drawing on a Middle, rather than an Old, English text, W. S. Merwin's recent version of *Sir Gawain and the Green Knight* (2002) is also notable in that it attests to the continuing influence of medieval literature on English-language poets into the twenty-first century.

Among this collection of poets stands Geoffrey Hill. It is Hill who most extensively grapples with the problems that arise from trying to connect with historically remote Anglo-Saxon England. In *Mercian Hymns* (1971) Hill ultimately questions the desire to view the Anglo-Saxon past as the origin of modern Britain as it occurs in the works of Pound or Bunting. This is a complex struggle because on one hand Hill recognizes the importance of remembering the past; if nothing else, his poem succeeds in drawing our attention back to Anglo-Saxon England and forces us to consider its relevance. On the other hand, Hill emphasizes the disparity between present-day Britain and medieval England. Through linguistic dissonance and extensive employment of anachronisms, Hill's poem showcases the historical dislocations that result from appropriating an Anglo-Saxon origin. Much of Hill's critique of the impulse to draw on the past to define the present remains well below the surface of his dense work and the reader must apply some degree of hermeneutical attention to tease out meaning in *Mercian Hymns*. Nevertheless, with a careful reading of the poem many indications of Hill's dubiousness emerge. Hill's disdain for imperial Britain is evident in another long poem of his from the same period, namely "An Apology for the Revival of Christian Architecture in England" (1978). As Jonathan Bolton points out, in this poem Hill is motivated by a need for "atonement" for British involvement in India.[3] With *Mercian Hymns* and "An Apology," Hill presents himself as a writer well aware of the historical grievances that can be leveled against his homeland.

Consisting of thirty short sections which resemble prose poems, *Mercian Hymns* takes a form reminiscent of Old English poetry as written by Anglo-Saxon scribes who wrote from margin to margin without the lineation of the metrical line we expect today.[4] Hill's poem evokes eighth-century England, particularly as it is figured through the memorable King Offa (757–96). Offa is well known for his advances in coinage,[5] defensive works (a dyke along the Welsh border still visible today), and legal codes, if not his contributions to the arts (some speculate that *Beowulf* ought to be credited to his court[6]). He is often celebrated for supplying much needed order to England during his time.[7] Despite his contributions to the security and prosperity of his homeland of Mercia, Offa is known for barbarous ways with his enemies, a quality which also receives attention in *Mercian Hymns*. The poem's depiction of the merciless nature of Offa indicates Hill is up to something different in his poem than his predecessors. After all, if he wished to promote Anglo-Saxon origins of his nation why would he choose a rather unlikable ruler as an originary figure whom he depicts as short tempered and intensely paranoid, a character whom he notes is "cushioned on a legend"?[8] These, surely, are not the characteristics Hill would like to see at the source of his native culture. Attempts to return to the origin typically entail striving to "bring something back" (to use Eliot's phrase) which is desirable, not bringing back the undesirable.[9]

Hill examines the figure of Offa in the "Acknowledgments" that he originally publishes with the poem (this section has been subsequently dropped in recent printings). Hill carefully stresses the ubiquity of Offa's presence, across the ages:

Chapter Four

> The historical Offa reigned over Mercia (and the greater part of England south of the Humber) in the years AD 757–796. During early medieval times he was already becoming a creature of legend. The Offa who figures in this sequence might perhaps most usefully be regarded as the presiding genius of the West Midlands, his dominion enduring from the middle of the eighth century until the middle of the twentieth (and possibly beyond). The indication of such a timespan will, I trust, explain and to some extent justify a number of anachronisms.[10]

I want to look into the "anachronisms" Hill speaks of here shortly. For the moment it is important to mark Offa's enduring influence, a figure through whom a notion of an essential "Englishness" has been implied by Hill's characterization of him as a "presiding genius of the West Midlands." Yet this is a phrase in which we must detect some irony: what does it say about England if a ruler of such ruthless character is its "presiding genius?" In the phrase "his dominion" one hears the language of tyrannical rule and this provides a further clue as to Hill's point of view. As Hill indicates in this passage, *Mercian Hymns* operates as a meditation on the possibility that Offa's influence persists to the present day and "possibly beyond." The logical conclusion to this line of thinking is that if Offa is the originary figure of Britain, that which is deplorable in him is also part of its origin. In chapter 1 I noted that John B. Vickery stresses the "elegiac" mood of modernism.[11] One way for Hill to combat the nostalgia for the past in predecessors like Eliot and Pound is to emphasize originary thinking's negative side—if Offa is the origin of Britain, he is the origin of its tendencies toward violence and imperialism.

Hill's critics have seen Offa as representative of the British nation in *Mercian Hymns*. William Logan contends that he is "a figure whose achievements in coinage and brutal political union continue to preside over notions of Britain as a nation-state."[12] Vincent Sherry concurs: "The historic Offa stands on the edge of the canonical British past, an inceptor in the nascent political life of the nation."[13] Henry Hart argues that Hill's poem is "an indictment . . . of a particularly English inheritance" and emphasizes Hill's role in this "indictment": "*Mercian Hymns* is a diagnosis of a king and his nation (Offa *is* the English nation) and Hill is the surgeon . . . to cut open the body, discover the sickness, and administer the cure."[14] I suggest that Offa stands as a synecdoche for the problems that come with the search for the origins of the nation.[15] This gets at one of the main issues involved in origin seeking. If one chooses to engage in originary thinking, how does one evaluate the drawbacks that inevitably come with the advantages of positing an origin (the advantage being, apparently, finding prestige for the present in the illustrious past)? Among modernist works this question often goes unanswered but it is a consistent problem for postmodernists. For example, Schwerner's *Tablets*, as we saw in chapter 2, looks into the ramifications of projecting a modern(ist) consciousness onto archaic texts. Similarly, Hill alludes to the search for the origin of the British nation by ironically gesturing to the "long-unlooked-for mansions of our tribe" in *Mercian Hymns* (NCP, 96). And like Schwerner, Hill considers how the past might have been viewed by his literary precursors. Reading Hill's poem against statements like Pound's self-proclaimed search for an "indigenous art" allows us to recognize Hill's response to the search for the origins of a national character evident in many modernist works.[16]

The nation proves, perhaps surprisingly, a relatively recent area of scholarly inquiry.[17] One of the most frequently cited examinations of the nation is Benedict Anderson's *Imagined Communities*. As his title implies, Anderson sees the nation as "an imagined political community" which he stresses is "imagined as both inherently limited and sovereign."[18] Anderson calls this an "imagined" community because the people of a nation are dispersed over a wide area and it is only through shared beliefs that they can identify with one another. His theory thus calls for a certain homogeneity of perspective which will be scrutinized by others. Anderson says this imagined community is "limited" because there are "finite, if elastic, boundaries, beyond which lie other nations."[19] Hill toys with this notion of the geographical boundaries of the nation

Chapter Four

in *Mercian Hymns*. Finally, Anderson stresses the "sovereign" nature of the community because "the concept was born in an age in which Enlightenment and Revolution were destroying the legitimacy of the divinely-ordained, hierarchical dynastic realm."[20] Hill similarly points out the difference between Offa's kingdom and the British nation. In Anderson's view, the nation is an historically-bound concept, one which came into being only with the confluence of two important factors: the advent of advanced capitalism and the establishment of print culture. He explains that "[T]he convergence of capitalism and print technology on the fatal diversity of human language created the possibility of a new form of imagined community, which in its basic morphology set the stage for the modern nation."[21]

Homi K. Bhabha has extended Anderson's point of view. He speaks of the "nation as a form of narrative" and, indeed, Hill can be seen as producing his own narrative of the British nation. This is a narrative which questions originary thinking by exposing the compromises which result from adopting it, particularly in having to accept the undesirable aspects of the origin (Offa's ruthlessness) with the desirable (Offa's social works). Hill's poem is unique among late twentieth-century long poems in the way it brings consideration of the nation to our attention. Bhabha points out that constructing the nation and national identity can be viewed as a textual process:

> To encounter the nation *as it is written* displays a temporality of culture and social consciousness more in tune with the partial, overdetermined process by which textual meaning is produced through the articulation of difference in language; more in keeping with the problem of closure which plays enigmatically in the discourse of sign.[22]

Bhabha's interest in "textual meaning," "the articulation of difference in language," and "the problem of closure" all point to a poststructuralist perspective on the instability of the signifier which ultimately serves to disrupt the concept of the nation that appears relatively unified in Anderson's paradigm. The instability of the discourse of nation, a discourse upon which the idea of the nation is built, points to a corresponding instability in the nation itself. Throughout Hill's poem there is a curious mixture of different levels of diction which resists a unified style that would be more felicitous in "narrating" his nation. His distrust of the signifier, in other words, is a reflection of his resistance to the kind of cultural unity that a view of British national origins in Anglo-Saxon England promises.

Elsewhere Bhabha speaks of "the ambivalence of the 'nation' as a narrative strategy."[23] He continues: "As an apparatus of symbolic power, it produces a continual slippage of categories."[24] It is thus against the relatively homogenous view of Anderson's problematic "imagined community," which assumes a commonality amongst its members, that Bhabha stakes his claim. Bhabha points to the dissenting voices of minorities and other marginalized figures within a nation as a group contrary to the unity of the nation as a single, monolithic entity.[25] Certainly Geoffrey Hill, despite an economically humble childhood, cannot be considered a marginalized figure in the same sense Bhabha discusses; in fact given his current, elevated status in the literary world many would consider him firmly planted in the center, not along the margins.[26] Nevertheless, Hill can write against Anglo-Saxon England as the inevitable national origin of Great Britain. In the manner of the figures Bhabha discusses, Hill offers a narrative of Anglo-Saxon origins filled with "ambivalences"[27] and "slippages" which allows him to distance himself from his literary precursors. In other words, Hill is not necessarily against Anglo-Saxon England itself but rather the idea of making it into an origin so prevalent in those who came before him.

Hill's postmodern response to the quest for an Anglo-Saxon origin evident in figures like Pound comes as little surprise when the historical situation Allen Frantzen describes in his book *Desire for Origins* is taken into consideration. Frantzen shows the institutional study of Anglo-Saxonism to be a byproduct of British involvement in the East. Building on the efforts of Edward W. Said

Chapter Four

(whose work I touched on briefly in the last chapter), Frantzen suggests British Orientalism inspired a search for the origin of some essential "Englishness" to stand in contradistinction to the foreign cultures with whom Britain was in commerce. Frantzen emphasizes "a central characteristic of Orientalism" which he notes is "an acute consciousness of the superiority of Anglo-Saxon heritage without which the stereotypical British view of India would have been inconceivable."[28] He argues that "the search for origins is never disinterested; those wishing to trace an idea or tradition to its historical, linguistic, and textual beginnings have always done so with a thesis in mind, and the origin they have found has often been an origin they have produced."[29] It is precisely this deliberately constructed nature of the origin which Hill evaluates in *Mercian Hymns*.

The search for origins among Britain's Anglo-Saxon past, then, can be viewed as contributing to the development of a British national character and ultimately reinforcing a notion of the superiority of the British nation. Frantzen remarks, "Nineteenth-century Anglo-Saxonists demonstrated the nationalism that motivated their scholarship; nationalism recalls in many ways the theological and political conditions in which Anglo-Saxon scholarship began in the Renaissance."[30] Concerning nationalism generally, Ernest Gellner notes, "Nationalism is not what it seems, and above all it is not what it seems to itself. The cultures it claims to defend and revive are often its own inventions."[31] Gellner's emphasis on the "invented" nature of "cultures" echoes Frantzen's statement that origins are always "produced." Eric Hobsbawm similarly notes, "[T]he national phenomenon cannot be adequately investigated without careful attention to the 'invention of tradition.'"[32] "Invention" is clearly the operative word for both Gellner and Hobsbawm. The emphasis on "invention" points to the arbitrariness and instability of tradition, how it is fabricated for specific, motivated reasons. What we find when we look into the search for Anglo-Saxon origins, then, is an invention of a tradition, namely Anglo-Saxon England as the origin of the modern British nation, that strengthens the image of the nation projected in contradistinction to the

"Oriental" Other. It is against this Other that Frantzen feels early Anglo-Saxon scholars defined themselves.

With the motivated nature of pursuits of tradition and origins in mind, I will now look more deeply into *Mercian Hymns*. Although there would be obvious advantages to dividing up my discussion of the *Hymns* thematically, I would prefer to work through the poem as it is sequenced. The advantage to this approach is that it allows us to observe the way in which the text progresses, from the invocation of Offa in the first section to his dissolution into thin air in the last, as if his spirit has been exorcised through Hill's "narration." Hill employs a dissonant diction and playful anachronisms to emphasize the disparity between the (post) modern and the medieval. This is a process which recognizes the "invented" nature of "tradition" and questions a national originary moment. The poem goes far to illustrate how dubious the results can be when attempts are made to bring Offa into the present time. I will finish my discussion with a brief overview of "An Apology for the Revival of Christian Architecture in England" which offers a somber view of Britain's status in the world after its long history of cultural and economic hegemony.

Language and Anachronism in "Mercian Hymns"

The very first of the *Hymns* presents us with one of the anachronisms Hill speaks of in his "Acknowledgement" section. The poem begins with an invocation of Offa that proves a strange mélange of the past and present: "King of the perennial holly-groves, the riven sandstone: overlord of the M5: architect of the historic rampart and ditch" its speaker intones (*NCP*, 93). Harold Bloom objects to Hill's assessment of the poem's anachronisms, noting, "Nothing can be anachronistic when there is no present."[33] Yet there is a tangible present in Hill's poem: that of the M5 highway which divides what was once much of Offa's Mercian kingdom. In its second definition for the term, the *OED* says an anachronism is "[a]nything done or existing out of date; *hence*, anything which was proper to a former age, but is, or, if it existed, would be, out of

Chapter Four

harmony with the present." That which is "out of harmony with the present" here is Offa as "overlord of the M5." Completed in 1977, the M5 links Birmingham and Exeter, in essence running parallel (although to a further degree southward) to the "historic rampart" Offa built on the Welsh border.[34] There is the sense, of course, in which Offa was lord over the region much of the road covers and thus, historically-speaking, he would be its overlord. However, discrepancies in technology make Offa appear unconvincing as the "overlord" of the M5: the modern highway system that webs Britain contrasts strikingly with the non-technological and archaic (even if effective) dyke Offa built. The historical parallel of the dyke and M5 breaks down on further examination: the M5 is intended to encourage travel; the dyke to inhibit it. Nevertheless, the passage presents Offa as an "architect" of not only the "historic rampart and ditch" which helped determine the Welsh border in Anglo-Saxon England, but also hints at the way Offa has been depicted as an early "architect" of the later English nation, as Logan and the others suggest.

The anachronism present in the first section of *Mercian Hymns* is only the first of many that persist throughout the poem. Others will follow this pattern of pulling Offa into the present for the purpose of contrasting his time with our own. The poem's very next section continues this promiscuous mixing of past and present. Here Offa's name is expressed as a "[b]est-selling brand" (*NCP*, 94) which strikes the reader as ironic, because if anything the name seems exotic and unfamiliar, contrary to what one would expect from a "best-selling brand." The originary nature of Offa's reign is noted in the poem's next sentence: "The starting cry of a race. A name to conjure with" (*NCP*, 94). Indeed "Offa" is a name Hill can "conjure with," thereby drawing attention to the Anglo-Saxon King's achievements which are sometimes figured as a "starting cry of a race" of the English people. But clearly this originary moment is also something which can be converted into a modern commodity (rendered as a "best-selling brand"). Traces of ambivalence thus begin to appear in the poem: even as he questions the desire to view Offa as a source of Englishness, Hill must take into account his own time and his own motivations for doing so (which appear to have something to do with addressing the commercial nature of contemporary life in this second poem of *Mercian Hymns*). There is a doubling of the irony here: not only does Hill appear to critique the desire to generate origins implicit in arguments about the relevance of Anglo-Saxon England, but he must also question his own attempt to write a poem which critiques origins. After all, even if Hill disregards Offa as a "starting cry of a race," he has still been considered as such by virtue of Hill's critique. Ultimately, the use of commercial culture in the poem, as with anachronisms, proves a means of promoting the differences between Offa's age and the present era.[35]

As Hart argues, this second hymn contains a series of puns and half-rhymes that make light of Offa's name.[36] The hymn begins: "A pet-name, a common name. Best-selling brand, curt graffito. A laugh; a cough. A syndicate. A specious gift. Scoffed-at horned phonograph" (*NCP*, 94). In his notes, Hill cites a source which represents "Offa" as a "'common name.'" Hart points to the repetition of sounds here—"graffito," "laugh," "cough"—which all mimic the sound of "Offa."[37] These terms cast a weak and ineffectual image of Offa: whether being poked fun at ("a laugh"), seen as compromised in health ("a cough"), or made the subject of an illicit inscription ("graffito"), no king would want to be associated with these terms. Hart mentions the other negative words that Offa's name invokes: "offal," "awful," etc.[38] The phrase I reviewed earlier, "[t]he starting cry of a race," can also be read as pun: what is the starting cry of a race? "They're offa!" This section reflects a concentration on the polysemic nature of language which, like anachronisms, will be a recurring motif in the poem. The effect of this consistent wordplay is ultimately to represent a breakdown in the signifying capacity of the signifier. The continual slippages of language, the by-default medium of the poem, finally renders the poem itself unstable.

Critics have commented on the childlike psyche Hill imbues Offa with.[39] A conflation occurs between the speaker's childhood memories and those imagined by Offa. Through this process, the

Chapter Four

present of the poem's speaker becomes Offa's present. In this way Hill offers an illustration of the manner in which ancient figures are made to inhabit the present, a procedure which casts them in our image (as occurs in Schwerner's poem from chapter 2). This conflation is present most notably in section VII which extends a theme of the poem's first section by placing Offa in an automobile, bringing attention back to the M5:

> Ceolred was his friend and remained so, even after the day of the lost fighter: a biplane, already obsolete and irreplaceable, two inches of heavy snub silver. Ceolred let it spin through a hole in the classroom-floorboards, softly, into the rat droppings and coins.

> After school he lured Ceolred, who was sniggering with fright, down to the old quarries, and flayed him. Then, leaving Ceolred, he journeyed for hours, calm and alone, in his private derelict sandlorry named *Albion*. (*NCP*, 99. Hill's emphasis)

The violent nature of Offa is clearly represented in the second stanza where he "flays" his friend for what seems a rather benign act of losing a toy plane. As with the ironic notion of "Offa" as a best-selling product, the name "Ceolred" stands in sharp contrast to the contemporary scene in which the character is placed. Like Offa, Ceolred was a king of Anglo-Saxon England and thus he is a character with a "real" historic basis.[40] In Ceolred we find another Anglo-Saxon personage placed in a contemporary setting in *Mercian Hymns* to stress the potentially dubious nature of the appropriation of the past. The Anglo-Saxon King Ceolred is transmuted into a boyhood friend who is subject to the whims of a childlike Offa—not an impressive image of either king. If Hill wanted to stress the "kingly" nature of Ceolred he surely would have placed him in a more dignified position than Offa forces him to occupy. The exotic nature of the name "Ceolred" promotes the historical distance between the modern reader and the historical figure who is being evoked so that finally one cannot help but be made more acutely aware of the problems that come with importing the past into the present; one might say a temporal dissonance results from that which is "out of harmony with the present."

After his outbreak of punitive violence, Offa departs in his sandlorry—its "private" nature accentuates his importance. The name of the sandlorry—"Albion"—gestures to the argument that the historical King Offa's reign helped along the transition of Great Britain from the ancient and mythical "Albion" to the modern nation it is today.[41] "Albion" is also something of a poeticism in the history of British literature; one finds it persisting throughout a number of works across the ages.[42] The sandlorry recalls the automobile imagery present in the first poem. The automobile emerges as a symbol of false power and freedom in the modern world: it is a machine that Offa uses to flee the scene of his "crime" and thus leave behind the wrecked situation he has created. The other persistent image here, the invocation of Offa's coins, is significant because the coins are now underfoot, among "rat-droppings." As noted previously, Offa's coinage was an important element of his reign and the fact it is represented among detritus such as this suggests that even the achievements of kings are subject to the ravages of time and the natural world. The image acts as yet another reminder of the deep time that separates Offa from us: the only physical evidence left of Offa is a few forgotten and scattered coins. Representative of *Mercian Hymns* as a whole, this short poem illustrates the compression of time and space evident throughout the text. This compression mimetically gestures to the foreshortening of history which is the potential byproduct of originary thinking.

The next poem in *Mercian Hymns* reinforces Offa's violent nature. However, instead of employing the theme of movement introduced by the M5 highway and carried through in the sandlorry imagery, Hill places Offa in a single, static scene. Here Hill utilizes a diction which is heightened and itself seemingly anachronistic:

Chapter Four

> The mad are predators. Too often lately they harbour against us. A novel heresy exculpates all maimed souls. Abjure it! I am King of Mercia, and I know.
>
> Threatened by phone-calls at midnight, venomous letters, forewarned I have thwarted their imminent devices.
>
> Today I name them; tomorrow I shall express the new law. I dedicate my awakening to this matter. (*NCP*, 100)

The term "maimed" recalls section V of the poem where we find the line, "I who was taken to be a king of some kind, a prodigy, a maimed one" (*NCP*, 97). This sense of "maiming" might be seen as a product of Hill's worldview. Logan speaks of Hill's vision of a "fallen world," one in which afflictions persist. As this poem demonstrates, Offa's affliction appears to be an intense paranoia which is the result of his political position. Perhaps because of this political position, the last sentence in the quote is ironic: there will be no "awakening." Offa changes in no discernible way through the course of *Mercian Hymns* and the text closes when he finally "vanishes" at the poem's end (*NCP*, 122). Here, in hymn VIII, the modern, mundane reality of a "phone-call" contrasts with the elevated, "poetic" nature of the diction ("forewarned," "thwarted," "imminent devices"). This disjunctive approach to language asks the reader to reflect on the poem's medium and the manner in which it renders Offa's rage. To the extent that the language Offa uses draws attention to itself we are forced to recognize that language is an unstable medium. We might recall Bhabha's intention to "encounter the nation as it is written." As a product of text himself, Offa, in other words, is like the nation: always written, always a textual construction.

Later in *Mercian Hymns*, in section XVII, automobiles appear again. Since he has already traveled over the geography of England—over "Albion" in his sandlorry "Albion"—Offa is now in Europe, apparently on a mission to Rome:[43]

Hill's "Mercian Hymns" and "An Apology"

> He drove at evening through the hushed Vosges. The car radio, glimmering, received broken utterance from the horizon of storms . . .
>
> "God's honour—our bikes touched; he skidded and came off." "Liar." A timid father's protective bellow. Disfigurement of a village-king. "Just look at the bugger . . ."
>
> His maroon GT chanted then overtook. He lavished on the high valley its *haleine*. (NCP, 109. Hill's emphasis)

John Needham suggests the middle section of this poem be read as a childhood recollection of Offa—provided we assume, of course, Offa is a child of the twentieth century.[44] However, there is little reason to doubt Needham's reading and what it demonstrates is how far we must go to confer on Offa a modern interiority to make him appear "contemporary" in his outlook. Hill's diction again proves distracting, this time marked by the word "haleine" which he notes derives from *La Chanson de Roland*.[45] The poem's punctuation is an issue here as well: there is nothing more than a set of ellipses to indicate a change in scene to the middle stanza. This stanza clearly occupies a different space and time than the two stanzas which frame it. Significantly, Offa has traded his sandlorry for a sports car now, the vehicles apparently working as devices to represent his moods: the sandlorry's slow, methodical movement may have been well coupled to his melancholy after "flaying" his friend Ceolred, but now that childhood memories fly through his mind the sports car appears better matched to his reflective state. The extravagance of the sports car also serves as a symbol of the vanity and power that is evident in Offa's character in his dealing with Ceolred in poem VII and his unnamed enemies of VIII.

Hymn XVIII finds Offa apparently committing the violence he promised earlier in section VIII: "He willed the instruments of violence to break upon meditation. Iron buckles gagged; flesh

Chapter Four

leaked rennet over them; the men stooped, disentangled the body" (*NCP*, 110). After utilizing his "instruments of violence," Offa returns to his car and Hill's play with words minimizes the impact of the violent imagery which the previous passage evoked: "He wiped his lips and hands. He strolled back to the car, with discreet souvenirs for consolation and philosophy. He set in motion the furtherance of his journey. To watch the Tiber foaming out much blood" (*NCP*, 110). The playful side of *Mercian Hymns* that emerges in the wordplay on Boethius' *Consolation of Philosophy* (ca. 524) ("souvenirs for consolation and philosophy") distracts us from Offa's act of violence by calling on us to regard the flippancy of the pun on the title of Boethius' well known work.[46] Similarly, there are no such things as "discreet" souvenirs in modern society. Souvenirs are made to be kitschy reminders of a trip or experience; if anything they strive to be indiscreet.[47] Offa's "souvenirs" propel the reader back to the second poem and its emphasis on a "best-selling brand" and the rhetoric of modern commercialism. *Mercian Hymns* is particularly adept at forcing us to move between its different sections, looking for unities in theme and character. In this way the poem itself is the site of much traversing, textually, as we attempt to extract meaning from the densely-packed hymns. The poem is ultimately against unity, however; whether it is unity of time (as figured in the anachronisms) or unity of discursive style (as in the language I have examined) the poem resists unification.

As with the hymn of Offa's phone-call, the diction in XVIII is humorously elevated in its final two lines: "furtherance" comes from a higher register of speech than the rather common phrase "he set in motion" and "much blood" must be considered in contrast to what, little blood?[48] Hill's speaker is intent on making every situation in which Offa appears finally seem ridiculous: whether his language (or the narrator's, as here) is pedantic and overwrought, or whether the focus is on locomotive imagery which stresses the anachronistic nature of using Offa as a figure of English origins—Offa as a maker of roads, as riding in his sandlorry after mercilessly handling his friend, as remembering a childhood biking accident while zooming down the highway in his maroon GT, or in returning to his car after another act of senseless violence—Offa's "kingly" nature is only evident in the merciless power he does not hesitate to use. There is something undeniably humorous about placing a medieval king in a modern automobile, a juxtaposition of the past and present that is anything but "harmonious." Moreover, few of the Anglo-Saxon King's entourage seem to have made the time warp with him: aside from the men who help him commit his violence in hymn XVIII, menial tasks, like driving a car, he performs entirely by himself. This suggests a certain lowered status for Offa when he is brought into our time, an expression of doubt in his importance.

In order to accentuate the disparity between Offa's wealth and power and the reality of more recent British social conditions, particularly in the fallout of the Industrial Revolution, a moving image of poverty is presented near the end of the poem in hymn XXV. XXV depicts the humble scene of a nailer's shop like one Hill's own grandmother labored in. The "I" here thus appears very close to Hill himself. The scene stands in sharp relief to the opulence of Offa, with his henchmen and striking sports car in XVIII. Though one of the longer of the hymns, XXV deserves to be quoted at length:

> Brooding on the eightieth letter of *Fors Clavigera*, I speak this in memory of my grandmother, whose childhood and prime womanhood were spent in the nailer's darg.
>
> The nailshop stood back of the cottage, by the fold. It reeked of mineral sweat. Sparks had furred its low roof. In dawn-light the troughed water floated a damson-bloom of dust—
>
> Not to be shaken by posthumous clamour. It is one thing to celebrate the "quick forge," another to cradle a face hare-lipped by the searing wire.

Chapter Four

> Brooding on the eightieth letter of *Fors Clavigera*, I speak this
> in memory of my grandmother, whose childhood and prime
> womanhood were spent in the nailer's darg. (*NCP*, 117)

E. M. Knottenbelt points out that Hill's allusion here is to John Ruskin's expansive "Letter to Workmen and Labourers of Great Britain," *Fors Clavigera*. As Knottenbelt indicates, the "eightieth letter" of the *Fors* presents an image strikingly similar to the one Hill presents of the speaker's grandmother in this section.[49] The term "darg"—which Hill glosses in his notes (following the *OED*) as "'a day's work, the task of a day'"[50]—comes from Ruskin's description. What Knottenbelt does not mention is that *Fors Clavigera* begins by expressing a desire to improve the British nation itself. In the second paragraph of his first letter, Ruskin describes Britain as being "afraid of the Russians; afraid of the Prussians; afraid of the Americans; afraid of the Hindoos; afraid of the Chinese; afraid of the Japanese" for the reason that "our only real desire respecting any of these nations has been to get as much out of them as we could."[51] In Ruskin's mind this deplorable foreign policy is reflective of the problem that "we have not courage to defend the right, when we have discerned it."[52] A few pages later, he writes, "I am sure it will be beneficial for the British nation to be lectured upon the merits of Michael Angelo, and the nodes of the Moon. But I should strongly object myself to being lectured on either, while I was hungry and cold."[53] Ruskin's indignation with the current state of the nation proves a useful analogue for Hill who similarly seeks to question the way in which the nation is figured in his reader's imagination. Like Ruskin, Hill will express regrets for Britain's imperialistic endeavors in "An Apology for the Revival of Christian Architecture in England."

The disparity between the mean working conditions of the workers of the nailer's shop and the excesses of Offa proves the most instructive comparison in the poem. The depiction of the woman spending her "childhood and prime womanhood" in the nailer's shop is antithetical to the image of Offa driving freely in his maroon GT: the dangers of the nailer's trade contrast with

Offa's memories of the relatively innocuous bicycle wreck he had as a boy. Hill is careful, however, to resist over-romanticizing the grandmother's condition; in fact her labor is rendered in images that stress the harsh reality of her working conditions ("reek of mineral sweat," "face harelipped by searing wire"). Given his recognition of the hardships of the nailer's trade, one cannot say Hill calls for a return to the days of pre-modern cottage industry. If anything, the hard work of the grandmother stands in contrast with the nonchalance and affluence of King Offa; this contrast does not promote the glories of nineteenth-century Britain over Anglo-Saxon England. Both periods are clearly filled with their own dangers and difficulties. The twentieth century is marked by problems particular to it as well; after all, its intense need for a connection with the past is the locus of Hill's meditation in the poem.

It might say as much about our habits of reading as it does about the section itself that this hymn is often considered Hill's most successful and affecting.[54] This surely has much to do with the relative ease with which it is read—it is markedly less dense than many of the *Hymns*—but also because it eschews the ironic anachronisms and disunity characteristic of most of the poems depicting Offa. Clearly this section does not need to qualify itself as the others do: its relatively cogent portrait of the speaker's grandmother laboring in the nailer's shop is locked in a specific time and place. It is an image apparently built from living memory and thus its realism frees it from the ironies—or extravagant diction—of many sections of the poem centered on Offa alone. The repetition of its stanzas ("Brooding on the eightieth letter . . . ") also helps to give it a greater sense of closure than most of the hymns offer. This repetition recalls the formulaic nature of two poems that survive from the Anglo-Saxon period: "Deor" and "Wulf and Eadwacer." Alluding to Old English verse does not render Hill beholden to the past, mainly because he only hints at its elements by his repetition and use of internal alliteration in the stanzas ("damson-bloom of dust"). This is a step removed from replicating or imitating past poetics, strategies which betray an attempt to return to the origin as in the overwrought line "Nathless there knocketh now" in Pound's "Seafarer," to cite only one example.[55]

As *Mercian Hymns* reaches its end, section XXVIII offers a nearly panoramic view of the past that sweeps over several epochs in England's history. Its first stanza represents the most basic of enduring concerns, the importance of familial ties:

> Processes of generation; deeds of settlements. The urge to marry well; wit to invest in the properties of healing-springs. Our children and our children's children, o my masters.

The hymn then widens its perspective:

> Tracks of ancient occupation. Frail ironworks rusting in the thorn-thicket. Hearthstones; charred lullabies. A solitary axe-blow that is the echo of a lost sound.
>
> Tumult recedes as though into the long rain. Groves of legendary holly; silverdark the ridged gleam. (*NCP*, 120)

The section pulls many of the images of earlier hymns back into view. For instance, the "groves of legendary holly" evoked in this passage recall the first section of the poem which named Offa "King of the perennial holly-groves."[56] Thus from prehistoric, pre-Christian time ("groves of legendary holly"), to the Roman era ("ancient occupation"), to the industrial age ("frail ironworks"), within a few lines Hill is able to evoke several major eras in English history. The idea that links these disparate periods is their subjection to the ravages of time, which yields only "tracks" of "ancient occupation." The reader is also reminded of the childhood reveries of the speaker and Offa by the mention of "our children and our children's children." But unlike Offa's foggy memories, the speaker looks forward to the future, not back to the past. This focus on Britain's future generations looks beyond Offa. In fact, at this point in the text Offa has begun to disappear from view: in the penultimate poem we are told "[H]e entered into the last dream of Offa the King" (*NCP*, 121).

The process of Offa's dissipation continues. In the final poem "he vanished" into thin air and "left behind coins, for his lodging" (*NCP*, 122). Offa's "lodging" occurs as much in Hill's mind as anywhere else. But if Hill is seen as "conjuring" Offa, as the second poem says, he must also dispel Offa's spirit at some point and this comes with emphasizing Offa's proper "lodging" in *our* imagination. His poem assesses the veracity of viewing Offa as an inadvertent originator of the English nation. Ultimately the poem forces us to think of Offa as a figure strictly of his own time and motivations. The poem has proven a mediation on the problem of engaging the past in a meaningful way by a singular psyche, one who bears striking resemblances to Hill at times (in particular in the *For Clavigera* poem). Hill has questioned the assumption that a return to the origin of Englishness will throw light on the present that we find in the statements of his precursors such as Pound and Bunting. Hart argues that Hill's poem is "an indictment . . . of a particularly English inheritance."[57] This is certainly true insofar as we see Hill's literary precursors serving as representatives of this "English inheritance." Hill's solution to the problem of literary origins is to take the work of Pound and Bunting to its logical extreme and show us how doubtful the results can be when we concern ourselves too much with defining the present by the past, by focusing too intently on what has been lost (in Vickery's sense of modernism's elegiac mood). Hill's findings are not unlike Schwerner's in that we are offered an illustration of the effect of the modern mind projected onto a figure of the distant past. Like Schwerner, Hill uses textual play to draw attention to this process of "modernizing" the historically-distant figure.

Yet we must not lose sight of the ambivalence at the heart of the poem. Offa should remain "lodged" in the mind, Hill implies, not necessarily as an origin of the modern British state, but instead as a figure of history whose presence is felt through an eroding dyke and some extant coins. Hill suggests that we should recognize the

Chapter Four

past, be cognizant of Offa's presence in British history, but the dangers of seeing him—and the Anglo-Saxon period—as the singular "origin" of modern Britain should be considered. I will now look briefly at Hill's poem "An Apology for the Revival of Christian Architecture in England" as a means of concluding this chapter. This poem provides a contrast with *Mercian Hymns'* ambivalence toward history. While "An Apology" is similar to *Mercian Hymns* in that it is dense and allusive, it nevertheless offers a clear condemnation of British imperialistic practices around the world.

Conclusion: "An Apology for the Revival of Christian Architecture in England"

Appearing in the volume following *Mercian Hymns* (*Tenebrae* [1978]), "An Apology" dramatizes "the conflict between commercial and national interests," as Jonathan Bolton writes. Comprised of thirteen sonnets, at its heart rests a series of sections subtitled "A Short History of British India." Here Hill takes a penetrating look at England's involvement in the East. Looking abroad where *Mercian Hymns* was concerned with domestic issues, the inspiration for "An Apology" appears to have been Hill's own trip to India. The speaker of its fifth sonnet asks: "Suppose they sweltered here three thousand years patient for our destruction." He ironically continues,

> Destiny is the great thing,
> true lord of annexation and arrears.
>
> Our law-books overrule the emperors.
> The mango is the bride-bed of light. Spring
> jostles the flame-tree. But new mandates bring
> new images of faith, good subahdars!
> ....
>
> Lugging the earth, the oxen bow their heads.
> The alien conscience of our days is lost
> among the ruins and on endless roads. (*NCP*, 144)

The "good subahdars" Hill mentions are named in the next poem: "Malcolm and Frere, Colebrooke and Elphinstone" (NCP, 145). Though apparently well-intentioned,[58] these men nevertheless represent the intrusion of an "alien conscience" that marks the cultural and economic infiltration of England into India. Bolton notes that the poem is "a plea for forgiveness" for this intrusion, and points to Hill's belief that "poetry can serve as an act of penitence." Indeed the irony which is such an important aspect of the poem—evident in the haughty "law-books" that "over-rule" the local rulers; that "they" waited patiently for "three thousand years"; that "destiny" of the kind that brought England into India is a "great thing," etc.—leaves little doubt where the speaker stands on cultural and political imperialism. As with *Mercian Hymns*, the speaker of "An Apology" feels it is the function of poetry to stand witness to, and comment on, public history in this way. If he cannot repair history, he can at least memorialize it so it is not forgotten.

Later in the sequence, the speaker's reflections on British-occupied India force him to take stock of the British nation itself:

> Platonic England, house of solitudes,
> rests in its laurels and its injured stone,
> replete with complex fortunes that are gone,
> beset by dynasties of moods and clouds.
>
> It stands, as though at ease with its own world,
> the mannerly extortions, languid praise,
> all that devotion long since bought and sold. (NCP, 148)

"Platonic England"[59] is bereft of its acquired provinces, a "house of solitudes" where the "complex fortunes . . . are gone," where integrity itself appears to have been up for sale ("all that devotion . . . bought and sold"). Yet England somehow finds itself "at ease with its own world," seemingly unable or unwilling to recognize its impoverished image. It is important to note that the "world" invoked is its "own," not "the" world, and this suggests a certain

Chapter Four

preoccupation with the self which Hill implies is a factor of British national identity—a self-centeredness quite readily observable with King Offa and which Ruskin also emphasized in Britain's dealings with other countries in the first letter of *Fors Clavigera*. Hill speaks with a sense of indignation and bewilderment, taking the only action he can in standing witness to Britain's historical injustices. In this pose he is more reminiscent of Irish writers like Ciaran Carson and Seamus Heaney than he is of British poets such as Bunting and Jones who were not motivated to write poetry of an overtly political nature.

In the poem's thirteenth and final sonnet, Hill incorporates religious imagery of a kind which is prevalent in much of his writing.[60] Here images of the natural world are mixed with a commentary on the diminished status of England, beginning with a first line which is tersely ironical:

> So to celebrate that kingdom: it grows
> greener in winter, essence of the year;
> the apple-branches musty with green fur.
> In the viridian darkness of its yews
>
> it is an enclave of perpetual vows
> broken in time. Its truth shows disrepair,
> disfigured shrines, their stones of gossamer,
> ....
> In grange and cottage girls rise from their beds
>
> by candlelight and mend their ruined braids.
> Touched by the cry of the iconoclast,
> how the rose-window blossoms with the sun! (*NCP*, 152)

The idea that Britain stands "as though at ease with its own world" from sonnet 9 controls "An Apology" up to its final lines. Logan's metaphor of Hill's "fallen world" is clearly present, a world in which "truth shows disrepair" and "disfigured shrines" persist. This scene sums up Hill's view of modern England: it is a nation marred by its impulse to colonize, tarnished even in the eyes of its own inhabitants. Its only hope, it would seem, is to somehow transcend its troubled past. The poem's final image, presumably an icon-breaker of Henry VIII's reign poised to smash the image of England's past (the rose-window), recalls the violence inherent in England's own history.

If Britain is projected as an "imagined community" as Anderson says, Hill's duty is to be a dissenting voice in the community and disrupt the homogeneous worldview suggested by Anderson's paradigm. The "cottage girls" who "rise from their beds/by candlelight and mend their ruined braids" depict the common people of England awakening to go about their work, despite England's historic misjudgments. Like the grandmother of *Mercian Hymns'* *Fors Clavigera* section, it is notably the cottage dweller, the economically downtrodden, who emerge as a source of inspiration for Hill—not the King, not the "good" subahdars. In the manner Bhabha describes, Hill "narrates" the British nation, clearly questioning its validity insofar as he feels the people of England (and elsewhere) have been made the victims of its machinations. Yet there is an underlying hope that persists. The image of the sun coming through the rose-window at "An Apology's" close indicates that the sun can still rise on Britain—even if it did finally set on the British Empire.

Knottenbelt points out the similar missions of *Mercian Hymns* and "An Apology":

> [The sonnets of "An Apology"] are not so much a reaction or qualification as a complement to [the] *Hymns*. There Hill's concern had been with his more personal roots; here, with an attempt to define his sense of poetry as a witness to his roots as an English poet. Both point towards and name origins, and show how he is marked by his past.[61]

I disagree with Knottenbelt's assessment that Hill's poem is about his "personal roots." As I have hoped to show, Hill is concerned with larger issues of the culture-wide appropriation of past historical moments as "origins"; he uses the personal only as a way to get at the public, and the poems are only vaguely personal. However, I am in perfect agreement with Knottenbelt's belief that "both [poems] point towards and name origins." The poems do in fact appear to be "complementary": where *Mercian Hymns* examines the results of not being mindful of our distance from the past, "An Apology" is a call to recognize the oversights of the past but also to move beyond them. Hill's work has continued to carry political motivations, although it has grown more recondite with a more rarified sense of humor in recent volumes such as *Speech! Speech!* (2000) and *The Orchards of Syon* (2002). Nevertheless, Hill is committed to producing a poetry that, while not necessarily being easily accessible, insists on an engagement with its cultural context. This is a poetry that throws light on our shared dilemma of how to use the past in a way that pays homage to important figures and periods but also refuses to elevate them beyond what is responsible. If Hill finally rejects originary thinking it is to free Britain to embrace its future and move beyond the grip of its past, to place its fate in the hands of "[o]ur children and our children's children." In my final case-study chapter, I will look into the ways in which Judy Grahn similarly overturns preoccupations of modernism, not in terms of national but rather cultural origins.

Endnotes

1 Ezra Pound, *Literary Essays*, ed. T. S. Eliot (New York: New Directions, 1968), 34.
2 Nicholas Howe, "Praise and Lament: The Afterlife of Old English Poetry in Auden, Hill, and Gunn," in *Words and Works: Studies in Medieval English Language and Literature in Honour of Fred C. Robinson*, ed. Peter S. Baker and Nicholas Howe (Buffalo: University of Toronto Press, 1998), 294–296.
3 Jonathan Bolton, "Empire and Atonement: Geoffrey Hill's 'An Apology for the Revival of Christian Architecture in England,'" *Contemporary Literature* 38.2 (Summer 1997). Ebscohost. 9 Feb. 2006 <http://web.ebscohost.com>.

Hill's "Mercian Hymns" and "An Apology"

4   Of course one could point to other prose poem traditions, especially that stemming from the French Symbolists. Nevertheless the Anglo-Saxon precedent has been viewed by Hill's critics (Henry Hart, *The Poetry of Geoffrey Hill* [Carbondale: Southern Illinois University Press, 1986], 156; Nicholas Howe, "Praise and Lament," 303) as the source of his form. Geoffrey Hill himself cites the prose "Mercian Hymns" from *Sweet's Anglo-Saxon Reader* as the inspiration for his poem (*Mercian Hymns* [London: Andre Deutsch, 1971], no page numbers).

5   Frank Stenton writes, "The continuous history of the English currency begins in Offa's time" (*Anglo-Saxon England*, 3rd ed. [New York: Oxford University Press, 2001], 223).

6   Sam Newton argues, "[A]lthough positive evidence is still wanting, there are grounds for regarding Beowulf as an eighth-century East Anglian composition" (*The Origins of Beowulf and the Pre-Viking Kingdom of East Anglia* [Cambridge: D. S. Brewer, 1993], xi). Along the same lines, Patrick Wormald notes, "*Beowulf* is undatable, and modern fashion favours a much later date than used to be accepted. But there remains a temptation to fit it into Offa's period, or that of his immediate successors. The poet seems to go out of his way to discuss Offa's illustrious namesake and claimed ancestor, Offa of Angen" ("The Age of Offa and Alcuin," in *The Anglo-Saxons*, ed. James Campbell [New York: Penguin, 1991], 128).

7   Wormald stresses Offa "was the first Anglo-Saxon king to be called 'king of the English' in reputable charters" ("The Age of Offa and Alcuin," 101). Of his international power, Stenton tells us that "Between 784 and 796 Offa was the only ruler in western Europe who could attempt to deal on equal terms with Charlemagne" (*Anglo-Saxon England*, 215).

8   Geoffrey Hill, *New and Collected Poems: 1952–1992* (New York: Houghton Mifflin, 1994), 105. Hereafter cited in the text as *NCP*.

9   T. S. Eliot, *The Use of Poetry and the Use of Criticism: Studies in the Relation of Criticism to Poetry in England* (Cambridge: Harvard University Press, 1964), 111.

10 Hill, *Mercian Hymns*, np.

11 John B. Vickery, "Frazer and the Elegiac: The Modernist Connection," in *Modernist Anthropology: From Fieldwork to Text*, ed. Marc Manganaro

(Princeton: Princeton University Press, 1990), 51.
12 William Logan, "The Fallen World of Geoffrey Hill," *New Criterion* 12.7 (March 1994). *Ebscohost.* 8 Feb. 2006. <http://web.ebscohost.com>.
13 Vincent Sherry, *The Uncommon Tongue: The Poetry and Criticism of Geoffrey Hill* (Ann Arbor: University of Michigan Press, 1987), 126.
14 Hart, *The Poetry of Geoffrey Hill*, 153; 154. Hart's emphasis.
15 Theorists of nationalism often posit England as the "origin" or first of nations. For an overview of theories of nationalism that start with the emergence of England's nationhood, see Phillip Spencer and Howard Wollman, *Nationalism: A Critical Introduction* (London: Sage Publications, 2002), 30–33.
16 Aside from Pound and Bunting, one calls to mind especially the cultural nationalism that lies at the heart of work by major Irish figures such as W. B. Yeats and Lady Gregory. Their joint project to collect Irish folk tales can be seen as an expression of cultural nationalism, as can be the plays they wrote, such as Lady Gregory's *Grania* (1911) or Yeats' *Cathleen ni Houlihan* (1902), for the Irish National Theatre.
17 John Hutchinson and Anthony D. Smith write, "As an ideology and movement, nationalism exerted a strong influence in the American and French Revolutions, yet it did not become the subject of historical inquiry until the middle of the nineteenth century, nor of social scientific analysis until the early twentieth century" (*Nationalism* [Oxford: Oxford University Press, 1994], 3).
18 Benedict Anderson, *Imagined Communities: Reflections on the Origin and Spread of Nationalism*, rev. ed. (New York: Verso, 1991), 6.
19 Anderson, *Imagined Communities*, 7.
20 Anderson, *Imagined Communities*, 7.
21 Anderson, *Imagined Communities*, 46.
22 Homi K. Bhabha, ed., *Nation and Narration* (New York: Routledge, 1990), 2. Bhabha's emphasis.
23 Homi K. Bhabha, *The Location of Culture* (New York: Routledge, 1994), 140.
24 Bhabha, *Location of Culture*, 140.
25 Bhabha, *Location of Culture*, 158.
26 William Logan, however, points out that Hill "has forced the marginal

into our modes of attention, at the risk of seeming bizarre or merely idiosyncratic and therefore a figure of margins himself" (Logan, "The Fallen World of Geoffrey Hill," http://web.ebscohost.com).

27 David Perkins sees ambivalence at the heart of Hill's poetry and notes Hill's "lines typically embody an intense, complicated self-conflict, and knot into unresolvable ambiguity" (*A History of Modern Poetry: Modernism and After* [Cambridge: Belknap Press, 1987], 463).

28 Allen J. Frantzen, *Desire for Origins: New Language, Old English, and Teaching the Tradition* (New Brunswick: Rutgers University Press, 1990), 28.

29 Frantzen, *Desire for Origins*, xii.

30 Frantzen, *Desire for Origins*, 56.

31 Ernest Gellner, "Nationalism and High Cultures," in *Nationalism*, ed. John Hutchinson and Anthony D. Smith (Oxford: Oxford University Press, 1994), 64–65.

32 Eric Hobsbawm and Terence Ranger, eds., *The Invention of Tradition* (New York: Cambridge University Press, 1983), 14.

33 Harold Bloom, Introduction. *Somewhere is Such a Kingdom: Poems 1952–1971* by Geoffrey Hill (Boston: Houghton Mifflin, 1975), xxiii.

34 I derive this information on the M5 from Ian Smith, *M5 (Birmingham to Exeter)*, <http://euclid.colorado.edu/~rmg/roads/m5.html>.

35 This is the primary way I see Hill differing from Eliot, to whom he is often compared. For a comparison with Eliot, see Logan. Unlike Eliot's (in)famous repudiation of the "Shakespeherian [sic] Rag" in *The Waste Land*, Hill is much less worried about the encroachment of commercial culture than he is in the way imagery might persist in it. T. S. Eliot, *The Waste Land: A Facsimile and Transcript of The Original Drafts Including the Annotations of Ezra Pound*, ed. Valerie Eliot (New York: Harvest, 1971), 138.

36 Hart, *The Poetry of Geoffrey Hill*, 162–63.

37 Hart, *The Poetry of Geoffrey Hill*, 163.

38 Hart, *The Poetry of Geoffrey Hill*, 163.

39 Martin Dodsworth, "*Mercian Hymns*: Offa, Charlemagne and Geoffrey Hill," in *Geoffrey Hill: Essays on His Work*, ed. Peter Robinson (Philadelphia: Open University Press, 1985), 52; Sherry, *The Uncommon Tongue*, 126.

Chapter Four

40 Ceolred ruled Mercia from 709 to 716. He was followed by Aethlbald who ruled for forty-one years and who was then followed by Offa. Of Ceolred, Stenton tells us he was "a dissolute youth, who oppressed monasteries, and according to St. Boniface died insane. He was the last descendant of Penda to rule in Mercia, and his death in 716 ends the first phase of Mercian history" (*Anglo-Saxon England*, 203).

41 Nicholas Howe puts this well when he writes, "*Albion* is a dazzling pun here: an old Latin name for England but also for a now-defunct manufacturer of trucks. In that one word, Hill's themes collide: the violent history of the kingdom, the boy's reveries of power, the fading of English industry (the sandlory is 'derelict') . . . all of the immersion in historical and temporal density that is Hill's abiding subject in *Mercian Hymns*" ("Praise and Lament: The Afterlife of Old English Poetry in Auden, Hill, and Gunn," 302).

42 One finds it, for instance, in historically canonical works such as "Complaint to His Purse" by Geoffrey Chaucer (line 22); in *The Fairie Queene* by Edmund Spenser (Second Book, Canto X, line 62); in William Shakespeare's *Henry V* (Act 3, scene 5, line 14) and *King Lear* (Act 3, Scene 2, line 85); in *Don Juan* by Lord Byron (Canto 16, line 666); in "On Sitting Down to Read King Lear Once Again" by John Keats (line 9); and "Albion" as a figure in William Blake's personal mythology and as a trope in works such as *Visions of the Daughters of Albion*.

43 Offa maintained good relations with Pope Hadrian I. Stenton writes, "Even at Rome Offa seemed a real, though inscrutable, force in the international world" (*Anglo-Saxon England*, 215).

44 John Needham "The Idiom of Mercian Hymns," in *Geoffrey Hill*, ed. Harold Bloom (New York: Chelsea House, 1986), 83–84.

45 Hill, *Mercian Hymns*, np. Martin Dodsworth explains the tenuous nature of the associations here: "The incongruous phonetic link between 'GT' and 'chanted,' as though the machine evoked a pilgrim's chorus, is precursor to the greater incongruity present in the link between the entirely unheroic and unpaid-for emotional excess of the 'lavished' and the heroic excess paid for in lives of the *Chanson de Roland*, the sound of whose horn is evoked in 'haleine'—the link itself

being made possible only by the mediation of the phrase 'high valleys'" ("*Mercian Hymns*: Offa, Charlemagne and Geoffrey Hill," 59).

46 There is a connection with Anglo-Saxon England and Boethius: Alfred (King of West Saxons, 871–899) was credited with translating *Consolation*. Later, Chaucer would also translate it, and Queen Elizabeth I did so as well.

47 There is of course the possibility that Hill wants us to think of "souvenir" in another sense: the *OED*'s first definition calls it "[a] remembrance, a memory." Given his earlier invocation of the language of commercialism ("best-selling brand"), however, this reading seems less likely.

48 As Hill indicates in his notes, "To watch the Tiber foaming out much blood" comes from Virgil (*Mercian Hymns*, np).

49 E. M. Knottenbelt, *Passionate Intelligence: The Poetry of Geoffrey Hill* (Atlanta: Rodopi, 1990), 186–87.

50 Hill, *Mercian Hymns*, np.

51 John Ruskin, *Fors Clavigera: Letters to the Workmen and Labourers of Great Britain, Volume I* (Boston: Dana Estes & Company, no date), 3.

52 Ruskin, *Fors Clavigera*, 3.

53 Ruskin, *Fors Clavigera*, 9.

54 M. L. Rosenthal and Sally Gall. *Modern Poetic Sequence: The Genius of Modern Poetry* (New York: Oxford University Press, 1986), 300; Needham, "The Idiom of *Mercian Hymns*," 81.

55 Ezra Pound, *Personae: The Shorter Poems*, ed. Lea Beachler and A. Walton Litz (New York: New Directions, 1990), 61.

56 The holly-groves call to mind Celtic England and thus a pre-Offa time. W. S. Milne conjectures that the "holly-grove" here might remind the reader of *Sir Gawain and the Green Knight* (*An Introduction to Geoffrey Hill* [London: Bellew, 1998], 113).

57 Hart, *The Poetry of Geoffrey Hill*, 153.

58 Bolton notes, "[H]owever misguided, [they] worked to improve the education, agriculture, and health conditions and attempted to codify laws in accordance with Indian customs and religious doctrine" ("Empire and Atonement: Geoffrey Hill's 'An Apology for the Revival of Christian Architecture in England,'" <http://web.ebscohost.com>).

59 The phrase comes from the epigraph from Samuel Taylor Coleridge, from *Anima Poetae*, with which Hill begins his poem.
60 Religious imagery and themes are especially prevalent in Hill's first book, *For the Unfallen* (1959), but persist up to one of his most recent publications, *Speech! Speech!* (2000).
61 Knottenbelt, *Passionate Intelligence*, 246–247.

5

"A New Myth of Origin": Judy Grahn's *A Chronicle of Queens* and Popular Culture

Popular Culture and the Postmodernist Long Poem

Postmodernism is often seen as a marriage of the high and the low, the intersection at which elite and popular culture meet and intermingle, if not wholly collapse into one another. A recent study by John Storey suggests popular culture is the "invention" of "intellectuals" as a means to widen the gap between social classes.[1] Historically this is a division which coincides with the onset of literary modernism and it is against what Storey calls "modernism's cultural elitism" that postmodernism posits itself.[2] Although postmodernism's embrace of popular culture has been a problem for critics like Terry Eagleton, who admits a "negative" view of the phenomenon,[3] postmodern writers are often liberated by the integration of elements of popular culture into their works. As Storey asserts, the use of popular culture motifs by postmodernists helps them critique the "cultural elitism" of, and question the assumptions underlying, modernism's dubiousness toward "low" culture.

Chapter Five

The postmodern long poem has been particularly fertile ground for different forms of culture to take root. The monolithic "tale of the tribe" of modernism, to use Pound's phrase, has been tempered by a growing awareness among writers of the long poem's place in a culture which has little use for poetry.[4] Combining popular culture materials and motifs with the "high" culture form of the long poem permits postmodernists to bridge the perceived "Great Divide" (as Andreas Huyssen puts it) between the high and low.[5] A number of postmodern long poems might be cited in this regard. Kenneth Koch's ottava rima *Seasons on Earth* (1987), for example, uses Disney characters to complement his story of a Japanese baseball hero named Ko. Edward Dorn's *Gunslinger* (1975) is another outstanding example. This poem uses the conventions of '60s TV and movie Westerns at the same time it employs a largely satiric approach. Writers like Koch and Dorn indicate a shift has occurred in what could be viewed as source material in the long poem.[6] John Ashbery's early long poems "Europe" (1962) and "The Skaters" (1966) similarly use popular culture sources.[7] Popular forms of entertainment such as music, TV, film, and vaudeville are referenced in John Berryman's *The Dream Songs* (1969). For these poets the popular is used subversively to critique modernist assumptions about the proper subject matter of poetry.

One finds popular culture in another poet of the period: Judy Grahn. As a lesbian activist, Grahn has consistently strived to use popular materials to represent the "common" woman, as the title of a volume of her poetry attests.[8] Her work thus eschews the "difficulty" and "cultural elitism" of high modernism in favor of an idiom more accessible to the average reader. The reason for this approach is simple: Grahn seeks to alter our ways of thinking about the position women have occupied in society for millennia; through a poetry which repudiates the densely allusive and fragmented poetics of modernism she can more directly make her points and project herself as a woman re-writing history to "express herstoric narration," as she says.[9] In her *A Chronicle of Queens* project, Grahn's main strategy is to use archetypal and mythological female figures to offer a depiction of women antithetical to the subservient position they have until recently occupied (and perhaps still do). To date, two of the four promised installments of Grahn's *Chronicles* have appeared: *The Queen of Wands* (1982) a long poem centered on the recovery of a "Helen" figure from male-dominated history and *The Queen of Swords* (1987) a verse drama (although she speaks of it as a single poem[10]) that recasts ancient Sumerian myth in a contemporary setting. Since Grahn's gender- and sexuality-based poetics in *A Chronicle of Queens* has been well analyzed by critics,[11] my focus on the presence of popular culture motifs in this chapter considers a quality of Grahn's work that has yet to receive comment. As in Dorn, Koch, and the others, I see the extended use of popular culture in *A Chronicle* as a means for Grahn to distinguish her project from modernist precursors, in the process rejecting their cultural elitism and male-centered worldviews.

Myth in Judy Grahn

Before moving on to discuss Grahn's long poem and play, I want to pause for a moment and examine an element of her work I have already mentioned: its use of myth. Myth and popular culture meet in another notable long poem from the period, namely James Merrill's *The Changing Light at Sandover* (1982). Like Grahn, Merrill mixes high and low sources. *Sandover* is a vast exposition (over 500 pages) of the relevance of spirituality in contemporary society. Helen Sword's comments on Merrill's (and Sylvia Plath's) use of a kitschy product of popular culture—the Ouija Board—as a divinatory device has some bearing on my examination of Grahn:

> [The Ouija's] very status as a commercial object . . . could well explain its tremendous symbolic appeal for two poets appropriate to a literary generation caught between modernism's mythopoetic nostalgia and postmodernism's self-conscious romance with commodity culture. For both Merrill and Plath, the Ouija board functions as a sort of psychic leveller, a fulcrum balancing the

Chapter Five

prophetic pretensions and iconoclastic impulses of high and low cultures, respectively.[12]

Sword usefully points out the conflation of the "mythopoetic" leanings of modernism and postmodernism's interest in "commodity culture" in Merrill. I want to suggest that, comparable to what Sword sees in Merrill, Grahn employs both myth and popular culture motifs to take stock of the culture in which she lives. Like Merrill, Grahn integrates popular culture into her poetry at the same time she evaluates the function of myth in present-day society.

The "mythopoetic nostalgia" which Sword evokes and which Grahn and Merrill work against perhaps finds its defining moment in T. S. Eliot's advocacy of what he calls the "mythical method." In a 1923 review of James Joyce's *Ulysses*, Eliot writes:

> In using myth, in manipulating a continuous parallel between contemporaneity and antiquity, Mr. Joyce is pursuing a method which others must pursue after him . . . It is simply a way of controlling, of ordering, of giving a shape and a significance to the immense panorama of futility and anarchy which is contemporary history. It is a method already adumbrated by Mr. Yeats . . . Psychology . . . ethnology, and *The Golden Bough* have concurred to make possible what was impossible even a few years ago. Instead of narrative method, we may now use the mythical method. It is, I seriously believe, a step toward making the modern world possible for art.[13]

A preoccupation with myth figures largely in many canonical modernist works, especially in poems by W. B. Yeats, William Carlos Williams, and of course Eliot himself. It is noteworthy the way myth appears a refuge in Eliot's thinking, helping one to escape the "futility" and "anarchy" of the present.[14] Eliot draws attention to the continuities of history, what he terms a "continuous parallel between contemporaneity and antiquity" that myth offers. Ultimately, however, it is difficult to see how this "mythical method" makes the "modern world possible for art" except in accommodating the "mythopoetic nostalgia" that appears in the works of Eliot and others.[15]

The *OED* defines myth as a "traditional story, typically involving supernatural beings or forces, which embodies and provides an explanation, aetiology, or justification for something such as the early history of a society, a religious belief or ritual, or a natural phenomenon." If the myth seeks to "explain" or "justify" "the early history of a society" it can be seen as a statement on origins, a way to posit an origin or legitimize something being called an origin. Eliot's mythical method is a means of rationalizing the employment of themes or motifs which find their source in antiquity and thus confer authority on his point of view. Contrary to this, Judy Grahn feels she can re-envision myth so that it questions the origins of patriarchy and asserts a woman-based culture in the distant past. In her prose work *Blood, Bread, and Roses* Grahn declares, "I fashioned a new myth of origin."[16] I will look at the significance of this notion in *The Queen of Wands* shortly. Grahn's work rests on the assumption that she can present her own explanatory story (myth) of how a woman-exclusionary culture began (origin) that she must now work to usurp.

Grahn's impulse to rewrite conventional myths (particularly in *The Queen of Swords*) has inspired Sue-Ellen Case to coin the term "'neomythology'" to refer to the project of "'taking back the myths'" she sees operative in Grahn's work.[17] Neomyths retell old myths "from within a gynocentric tradition, tracing new histories for their mythological characters and narratives which result in an alternative interpretation of their symbology and meaning."[18] This work leads to a reinterpretation of history that evokes a matriarchally-based culture that fell with the rise of ancient Greece.[19] Myths, like origins in Grahn's view, are unstable and arbitrary; they can be changed, or replaced. Contrary to Eliot's metaphor, which I cited in my introductory chapter, to "return to the origin and bring something back" in his statement on the "auditory imagination," Grahn feels she can, indeed must, construct the origin herself; myth and popular culture—images of the past and

Chapter Five

the present, respectively—become two tools to use in this endeavor. The constructed nature of the origin is thus foregrounded in Grahn's *Chronicle* project.

"The Queen of Wands": The Goddess and Popular Culture

In many ways Grahn is very much of her time in that her work evokes a belief in a primary Goddess who was systematically replaced with the monotheistic male God of several of the world's major religions that survive today. The Goddess tradition received wide currency over the last century and a half. As Ronald Hutton has shown, archaeological work of the late-nineteenth and early-twentieth centuries exhumed, and sometimes fabricated, evidence for worldwide goddess worship which reportedly predated the establishment of male-centered societies.[20] The argument for an early goddess-based society gained popularity with many in the 1970s. One of its effects was to lead some to return to what they saw as originary religions, such as Paganism and Wicca, which elevated women to a status equal to, or eclipsing, that of men. Grahn's *Chronicle* integrates elements of these alternative religious and spiritual practices into its worldview. Perhaps most notably, sections of Grahn's *Chronicles* project are named after the Minor Arcana of the Tarot deck, reminiscent of the many occult-inspired literary works of the last several decades.[21] Occult themes persist throughout *The Queen of Wands*.

Robert Graves' *The White Goddess* (1948) remains an important text that bridges Eliot's mythical method and Grahn's later "neo-myths." One of the major modern statements on mysticism in poetry, Graves' book also advocates a goddess-centered literature. Grahn acknowledges the importance of *The White Goddess* in several places.[22] Graves believes that reflection on an originary goddess[23] can lead one to the source of "true poetry." He explains,

> My thesis is that the language of poetic myth anciently current in the Mediterranean and Northern Europe was a magical language

bound up with popular religious ceremonies in honour of the Moon-goddess, or Muse, some of them from the Old Stone Age, and that this remains the language of true poetry—"true" in the nostalgic modern sense of "the unimprovable original, not a synthetic substitute."[24]

A few pages later he concludes that his book is "about the rediscovery of the lost rudiments, and about the active principles of poetic magic that govern them."[25] His project, then, is one centered on recovering the origins of poetry in a culture coalesced around goddess worship. In Graves' view, a goddess-centered society is primary, an "unimprovable original," to which we must return. If Graves' book is about recovering lost knowledge it is also an effort, like Eliot's mythical method, to take "a step toward making the modern world possible for art" by reconnecting us with that which we have lost. Grahn's project differs from Graves' in the position from which each speaks: Graves is perhaps located on the margins of modernism, but Grahn is certainly located well beyond those margins. The belief in the immutability of myth in Eliot persists in Graves, whereas Grahn recognizes the arbitrariness of myth.

Although Graves looks to prehistory for evidence of the Goddess, Grahn traces an initial woman-centered culture back to ancient Sumer. In her Foreword to Betty De Shong Meador's recent translation of the Sumerian poet Enheduanna, Grahn reveals her mission to recover a forgotten woman-based literature. As Grahn stresses, Enheduanna is presumed to be the first identifiable poet of writing in history.[26] In her own *Chronicle of Queens*, Grahn presents a synthesis of disparate mythological traditions to show the ways in which images of women have persisted over time and across cultures. As part of her evidence for the overlap of mythological traditions, she stresses the linguistic similarities in the names of a number of goddesses in the section "Helen's Names" in *The Queen of Wands*. "Helen" becomes a synecdoche for women's plight in Western history. The poem begins,

Chapter Five

> Helen has such a lengthy history
> as a god and as a queen
> that her name, El-Ana, has derivations
> and echoes that are widespread over
> continents. The Muhammedan Venus is called
> Anael, which has the syllables of
> El-Ana reversed. From El comes Bella
> meaning "beauty."
> Beulah Ann is one variation,
> as are Helena, Helga, Holga, Helda,
> Hilda, Holde, Hillary, Helna, Hildegard,
> Helle. Hlin. Hlinda, Linda. Honnele. Heleme. (QW, 16)

And her list goes on.[27] It is significant that Grahn should mention "Hilda" as one of these names. It recalls Hilda Doolittle, better known as H. D., Grahn's acknowledged precursor and author of *Helen in Egypt* (1961) which I touched on briefly in chapter 1. H. D. is indeed something of a Helen figure for Grahn in that she represents a woman attempting to forge her own aesthetics even as she is dominated by a male-centered modernism.[28]

In the preface to her long poem, Grahn notes that she "first met the Queen of Wands in a 1913 translation of a clay tablet of ancient Babylonian writing" (QW, xii). Ancient Sumer is a watershed culture for Grahn because it provides the cuneiform tablet that supplies the inspiration for her poem and it serves as the origin for the divine female figure Grahn wishes to resurrect. Through this process Sumer becomes both an origin and an end in the sense that Grahn has to work her way back through time to reach it. "In investigating Helen's story I found an astonishingly worldwide myth of a female god of beauty, fire, love, light, thought, and weaving," Grahn writes, "She is a figure of many forms and names and countries, and she is the Queen of Wands" (QW, xii). I have already sampled one of the many lists of variant names of the Helen figure that Grahn incorporates into her works. She has little trouble embracing Carl Jung's belief in the persistence of archetypes, and indeed she makes reference to Jungian ideas in her work.[29] The Jungian paradigm of recurring archetypes over the course of human history provides Grahn with a philosophical structure she can use to elaborate her own version of myth.

To demonstrate the primacy of the Sumerian cultural moment, Grahn offers the 1913 translation, mentioned in her preface, of the "Tablet of Lamentation" rendered by Stephen Langdon. It clearly affords evidence of the historical oppression of women. "In my temple he pursued me, in my halls he terrified me," its speaker intones,

> Like a frightened dove upon a beam I passed the night.
> Like a sudin-bird that flees from a cranny I hastened by
>   night.
> From my temple like a bird he caused me to fly.
> From my city like a bird he caused me to fly. (QW, 9)

These lines work as historical evidence for Grahn's contention that women have been subjected to the dominance of men for millennia. She writes, "Moved by the tale told in the Tablet of Lamentation, I searched for other stories of stolen queens, wanting to identify this one with a name, occupation, some motive for the theft" (QW, xii). As her poem goes on, she will tie this systematic subjugation of women to the story of Helen of Troy to offer a comprehensive argument for viewing the history of the West as one built on gender inequity. Grahn's duty is to disrupt this division so that women return to a central position of power in society and cease to concern themselves with threats of violence from men like the one who terrifies the speaker of the "Tablet of Lamentation."

Despite the originary nature of the Sumerian materials, Grahn chooses to name her archetypal female figure "Helen" because of the image it evokes of a woman abducted by men who fight blindly and ruthlessly over her, all the while oblivious to her desires. As Grahn says, "The most persistently retold story of a queen stolen in Western tradition is that recounted in *The Iliad*" (QW, xii). The depiction of Helen in Homer's epic proves to be a defining moment in Grahn's "herstory." In her copious notes to *The Queen of Wands* she argues,

> In brilliant, world-influencing Egypt, the rulership passed through the female line and the economy was solidly in women's hands . . . men did much of the labor and craftwork while women did much of the management . . .
> The Trojan War represented a shift in power: the Greek soldiers who won took skilled labor, especially the valuable weavers, back with them as slaves. (QW, 104)

This historical shift—from an ancient Egyptian culture in which Grahn sees women retaining agency to a civilization in which they are made subject to the economic interests of men—is dramatized in the poem, notably in a soliloquy by Helen. Like H. D. before her, Grahn will offer a view of history from Helen's perspective. Helen remarks:

> I went out a Queen
> a Sovereign, Mother of my people
> and a lover—
> I came back a captive.
> My husband had gone out
> a King, a Sovereign
> and a soldier.
> He came back a tyrant,
> a master of slaves—
> and I came back a slave. (QW, 25–26)

The extent to which Helen speaks for herself, and possesses an interior life which she feels free to verbalize, distinguishes Grahn's character. The figure of H. D.'s *Helen in Egypt* does not display the same self-conviction that Grahn's does.[30] The diction used by Grahn's Helen is particularly revealing: terms like "captive," "tyrant," and "slave" certainly come from the language of enslavement and colonization. Grahn references the West's long history of domination of other cultures in the notes accompanying the poem (QW, 107–108). Her recognition of the theme of colonization in *The Queen of Wands* allows her Helen to be more attuned to the postcolonial concerns of the final decades of the twentieth century than H. D.'s figure who appears still to be trying to establish the individuation which Grahn's character is in the process of expressing. Grahn is able to build on H. D.'s work, in the process rendering a Helen who seems all the more "real" because of her contemporary point of view.

Yet the contemporary nature of Grahn's Helen has the potential to appear misguidedly anachronistic. Part of the purpose of Geoffrey Hill's depiction of the Anglo-Saxon King Offa in *Mercian Hymns* (1971), as evidenced in the last chapter, is to explore the problems that come with bringing an historical person into the present for the purpose of identifying an originary moment in the past. In *Mercian Hymns*, Offa is placed into a contemporary situation almost intact; I noted how attempts to confer a modern interiority on him finally appear ridiculous in the poem. By contrast with Hill's cautionary tale, Grahn promotes the persistence of the Helen figure, a figure who is certainly less defined (because she cannot be based on an historical personage like Offa) than Hill's character. Hill's Offa retains his kingly affectations when he enters the modern world, despite the disparity between his historically-distant England and the modern British nation he comes to occupy. Helen, however, acclimates herself to modern society, as I will show. This is not to say that Grahn is pleased with all aspects of current popular culture; in fact she often registers ambivalence. However, the purpose of her poem is not to examine the problems that follow in attempting to uncover an origin in the past as in Hill's case. Rather, as we have seen, she seeks to show that the origin can be constructed to correspond with the political motivations of the individual. Origins are always arbitrary in Grahn's view.

Through the course of *The Queen of Wands*, Helen is represented in a number of guises, from a weaver, to the Norse Frigga, to

Chapter Five

Sleeping Beauty, to Helen of Tyre. These different appearances offer Grahn a way of representing Helen through the ages and across cultures. Helen's persistence over time is emphasized in the poem: "I am the Queen of Wands," she says, "I am who stands/ who always will/and I am who remembers/the connections woven, little eggs/along the message line" (*QW*, 41). The "message line" here is presumably the literature that links Helen to Grahn, across centuries. Helen's importance is asserted to the point that she is made present at creation: "I remember giving dinosaurs/to the tall unfolded ferns to entertain them./and [sic] immortality to the cockroach/I remember the birthday of the first/flower" (*QW*, 41–42). Within a few lines Helen appears to have succeeded in replacing the traditional monotheistic male god as originator of life on earth with her own image. This is a clear example of Grahn expressing the "herstoric narration" she announces in the preface to her poem.

The element of popular culture I cited at the beginning of this chapter comes into view in Grahn's examination of Goddess imagery in contemporary society, in particular in film. Grahn explains her view of the plight of the female figure: "[Helen's] capture and her still-living presence is primary in Western tradition, from *The Iliad* to *Cinder Ella* to *Faust* to modern movies of tragic female stars who rise, fall, are murdered, rise again" (*QW*, 94). Grahn draws a parallel between the present and past in a way anticipated by Eliot's mythical method. However, for Eliot returning to myth was a corrective measure; for Grahn it is to emphasize how little things have changed since that early time when women were first subjugated by men. Her mention of "modern movies" highlights this point. Although film can engender images of victimized women ("tragic female stars who rise, fall, are murdered"), as we shall see, Helen's status as a film star can also be a source of empowerment in the agency that celebrity affords her.

The Queen of Wands' "Helen in Hollywood" is the poem's most straightforward examination of the way women are depicted in popular culture. Grahn describes the modern-day Helen: "She writes in red red lipstick/on the window of her body,/long for me, oh need me!/Parts her lips like a lotus" (*QW*, 46). The emphasis on cosmetics in these lines appears to parody the imagery found in popular culture projections of female beauty. This passage sustains Grahn's argument that women remain objects onto which men project their desires. However, in her book *Blood, Bread, and Roses* Grahn discusses the importance of cosmetics in ancient menstruation rituals.[31] She notes that "Lipstick . . . may be considered the first cosmetic" because cosmetics "began as simple signals of warning and instruction, enabling women to control how they were seen, whether they were avoided or approached. The woman didn't need to display her vulva, she could paint her mouth with menstrual blood."[32] She argues that the basis of contemporary society can be found in the way menstruation ordered civilization. She writes, "In considering menstruation as female power, in contemplating creation stories and the uniqueness of the human capacity for elaborating culture, I fashioned a new myth of origin."[33] With her self-conscious revelation of a desire to create a "new myth of origins" in mind, the lipstick can be viewed as a symbol of female power, the survival of a ritual from an older, woman-centered time, even if the line "long for me! oh, need me!" clearly bears traces of irony. This irony illustrates the ambivalence of much of the poem: there is the recognition that as she draws on her lipstick, Helen may not be aware of what she does, unlike her creator, Grahn, who painstakingly peers into the past to identify the cultural power Helen has lost without realizing it.

Reading the lipstick passage the reader also recalls the dedication of the book—"To Marilyn Monroe/who tried, I believe/to help us see/that beauty has a mind/of its own"—which does *not* appear to carry any hint of irony. If Monroe, as the over-sexualized image of the ideal American woman, seems odd for a dedicatee to such a clearly revisionist text, it may be because we fail to fully grasp Grahn's argument. It becomes clearer as the poem goes on. She writes,

> We infuse her.
> Fans, we wave at her

> like handmaids, unabashedly,
> we crowd on tiptoes pressed together
> just to feel the fission of the star
> that lives on earth,
> the bright, the angel sun
> the luminescent glow of someone
> other than we.
> Look! Look! She is different.
> Medium for all our energy
> as we pour it through her. (QW, 46–47)

Here again Grahn expresses ambivalence: on one hand she admires the strength of figures like Monroe who can act as a "medium" for "our energy," on the other regretting the way this individual is reduced to her parts ("her lips like a lotus") and who must be forced to bear the burden of being a "bright, angel sun" with a "luminescent glow" by her "fans."[34] Yet a few lines later in the poem, the speaker directly acknowledges our debt to this modern day Helen: "She is the symbol of our dreams and fears/and bloody visions, all/ our metaphors for living in America. // Harlowe, Holiday, Monroe // Helen/When she goes to Hollywood" (QW, 47). Helen's image, insofar as it is a "metaphor for living in America" performs an important function in allowing us to understand ourselves and to identify the values that underpin American society, even if one of those values appears to be a superficial obsession with physical beauty. For all the love of surfaces in American society, there persists the irony that the American "commodity culture" of cosmetics has its roots in ancient menstruation rituals. It is thus by being mindful of past practices that Grahn appropriates the power taken from women by men who presumably continue to be the decision makers in Hollywood and in the cosmetics industry.

In the final analysis, this Helen is decidedly greater than the sum of her parts. The poem's speaker stresses,

> She is far more than a product
> of Max Factor,

Grahn's "A Chronicle of Queens"

> Max Factor didn't make her
> though the make-up helps us
> see what we would like
> to take her for. (QW, 48)

What we should "take her for," in Grahn's estimation, is a figure with a multiplicity of identities, not all of them flattering:

> she who is princess and harlequin,
> athlete and moll and whore and lady,
> goddess of the silver screen
> the only original American queen
>
> and Helen
> when she was an angel
> when she went to Hollywood. (QW, 49)

The poem ends here; we do not find out, grammatically speaking, what happened "when she went to Hollywood." Nevertheless when the poet calls her "the only original American queen" Grahn recognizes the ways in which movies and the glamour-inspired entertainment industry might be guilty of perpetuating those historical grievances Grahn levels at Western society as aftereffects of the Trojan War. Yet the poet also attributes a certain agency to the role of being a "goddess of the silver screen." It permits a return to an elevated status which promises the possibility of being a "symbol" through which the reader can work his or her way into a future informed by the past. That is, if we identify both the subjugation of Helen and also her untapped power, we begin to recognize not only the cultural ills associated with her, but also that she has the potential for regaining the power she once possessed. It will be the work of *The Queen of Swords* fully to restore her to her former glory.

The volition emerging in Helen in the final lines of "Helen in Hollywood" is carried over into the last sequence of *The Queen of Wands* where cosmetics, as earlier in the poem, are appropriated as symbols of power. Its speaker, known only as "Annie Lee" (presumably another modern version of the name Helen[35]), declares, "This tube of lipstick/is *my* wand/this pencil and this emery board/this mascara applicator/brushing black sex magic . . . these knitting tools for/putting things together,/these are my wands" (*QW*, 89–90. Grahn's emphasis). These objects, commodities produced to impose a popular culture sense of beauty and domestic duty on women, are unexpectedly taken by the female speaker to be emblems of power. The emphasis on "black sex magic" and the transmutation of the "knitting tools" into magical wands brings the poem full circle in its interest in occult symbols. Here the occult (the "black magic") and the popular culture (the "tube of lipstick," etc.) motifs find a final, lasting image that unites them to the book's title: *The Queen of Wands*.

With its mixture of disparate sources that vary from imagery drawn from the cosmetics industry and movies to the persistence of women in traditional myths, *The Queen of Wands* sets the stage for the next installment of Grahn's *Chronicle of Queens*. *The Queen of Swords* will literalize what is generally only metaphorical in *The Queen of Wands*: Helen will continue to develop from the indignant, but still compromised figure in *The Queen of Wands* to one who secures an identity that symbolizes a reconstitution of women into positions of power in society in *The Queen of Swords*. A major difference between the two texts, however, is that *Swords* utilizes more formal play, a dominant characteristic of postmodern literature that is evident in a number of long poems from the latter half of the twentieth century.[36]

"The Queen of Swords": The Transformation of a Goddess

If *The Queen of Wands* maintains some distinction between the modern Helen who appears in popular culture personages like Marilyn Monroe and the Helen figure of ancient myth, *The Queen of Swords* represents a complete collapse of time and space in which the ancient, mythic Sumerian past paradoxically occupies

Grahn's "A Chronicle of Queens"

the present. The two eras are combined to produce something of an alternative reality in which sexuality is freer and uninhibited by patriarchal prohibitions.[37] This is not to say that one enters this "reality" at will. In fact, part of the purpose of the play is to show how the initially heterosexual Helen is converted into a realized individual as a lesbian through an intense struggle. There is an awakening in Helen, then, one which aids her in regaining the position of authority she once maintained; her sexuality is apparently a key to the self-realization that offers her power in modern-day society.

The Sumerian goddess known as Inanna becomes *Swords'* Helen figure. The play dramatizes Inanna's journey into the Underworld.[38] In the original tale, Inanna descends to the land of the dead to bolster her already considerable powers and emerges more formidable than before. However, as payment to Ereshkigal (the female deity in charge of the Underworld who permits this empowerment), Inanna must elect someone to take her place and this duty is finally divided between her husband, the bull god Dumuzi, and his sister, each of whom serve half of every year. For Grahn this myth recalls a time before women were enslaved (both literally and metaphorically) in the age of Homer. In her introduction to the play, Grahn relates Inanna to the Helen figure. She discusses the fallout of the Trojan War and notes Helen "ran for cover under the relentless authority of the all-male monotheism that gradually replaced her worship during these last few centuries" (QS, 1). She then observes "Helen did not really die . . . and will return to us when we are ready" (QS, 1). That the origin will somehow "return to us" echoes Graves' similar expression of hope, at the end of his book, that the White Goddess would reappear. Like Graves before her, Grahn will posit the importance of remembering in *The Queen of Swords* as a way to accommodate the return of an earlier, and presumably better, way of thinking. In fact *Swords* can be read as an allegory intended to illustrate the procedure by which the forgotten history of women can be recovered. The figure of Inanna/Helen is clearly presented as exemplary. She gains a better perspective on her past as the text progresses and draws on the strength of her female companions to help her complete her transformation.

The revisionary nature of Grahn's play becomes apparent in the change she makes to the setting of the ancient story. The Underworld in Grahn's tale is underground only in a metaphorical sense: it is a lesbian bar and Ereshkigal notes "Here in the belowworld Lesbians are loved,/and Lesbians love" (QS, 48). In *The Queen of Swords* the use of myth allows the present to be the site of the ancient as Eliot intimated in his comments on the mythical method, but certainly there is a new spin on an old theme here. The popular culture setting—or what might be better called a "subculture" setting, as Johanna Dehler suggests[39]—allows Grahn to bring myth into a situation that throws light on the present; not as an illustration of how "futile" and "anarchic" our current society is, as Eliot stated, but rather to permit us to recognize the ways in which we can improve our culture. The usefulness of Sue-Ellen Case's neologism "neomyth" in capturing the self-conscious reinterpretation of myth in *The Queen of Swords* is apparent in the new dynamic that a preoccupation with alternative sexualities brings to the ancient story. Grahn does not wish purely to resurrect the past but rather to embellish it with contemporary concerns.

A significant alteration to the content of Inanna's tale is that it is Dumuzi's girlfriend, instead of his sister, who shares his duty to remain in Ereshkigal's Underworld. Grahn explains that her adjustment to the earlier text is due to the nature of our "fragmented culture" which does not contain a situation equivalent to the original (QS, 167). However, it seems more likely that Grahn wishes to rationalize Inanna's dismissal of Dumuzi to the Underworld in her place. This action receives no real explanation in the original tale; instead Dumuzi seems unjustly punished for Inanna's greedy desire for greater power. In Grahn's version, Dumuzi's crime of infidelity is repaid with a fitting punishment, making the story's outcome more reasonable to modern readers and more consistent with her project to diminish the status of men so women are elevated to assume their positions of authority.

The play begins by representing Helen's feelings of ineffectualness. She laments: "A queen am I/Queen Helen is my office./Yet *trivial* is how I feel./Venus of what universe am I? (QS, 16. Grahn's emphasis). After her articulation of dissatisfaction with her current life is quietly dismissed by her husband, Helen decides to strike out on a "journey" (QS, 18). This journey takes her to the "Underworld" bar owned by Ereshkigal. Ereshkigal's characterization of herself to Helen emphasizes her ubiquity in popular culture: "[Y]ou've seen me glaring in fury from some picture/in the newspaper, taken in some jail, you've seen me/in the grade-B movies . . . I played your older/sister Clytemnestra once, in a violent Greek play (QS, 24–25). The reference to the "B movie," or the photo of Ereshkigal in jail, suggests the way she has been marginalized in contemporary society—we are in the presence of "Helen in Hollywood" no longer. This is not to say Ereshkigal fails to see the light of her situation: her presence in a second-rate movie appears to be worn as a badge of honor and at one point she calls herself the "Butch of Darkness"—an example of the kind of playful humor we will see more of momentarily (QS, 51). From "grade-B movies" to a "violent Greek play," Grahn has little difficulty moving from modern day kitsch (the B movie) to the "high" culture of ancient Greek tragedy; these distant points on the spectrum of products of culture coexist in Grahn's work with little conflict. For Grahn, as Edward Dorn says, "one thing [is] as good as another . . . as source."[40]

In contrast to the individuation and self-deprecating sense of humor Ereshkigal reveals in dubbing herself the "Butch of Darkness,"[41] Helen must work at gaining, or rather re-gaining, a distinct self-image. Over the course of the play Helen must be reminded of her former glorious place in pre-patriarchal culture which she has slowly forgotten over time. Ereshkigal tells Helen: "You were a goddess before Demeter's time,/Lady Venus of aboveworld form,/Inanna by name, Sumerian born—/you passed through seven gates of the underland/to deliver yourself into my hands,/into Ereshkigal's hands" (QS, 51). A number of characters enter the play solely to help Helen in this complicated process of remembering. The host of figures includes Amazon warriors who tell her, "Helen, your forces/are in the beauty of your memory" (QS, 69). The choice of the term "forces" here gestures toward the paranormal nature of Helen's powers appropriate to an ex-goddess and, in a more contemporary way, suggests occult practices that I have already noted to be the byproduct of goddess worship in our age. The term also evokes the image of a military formation, with Helen at its head, presumably assembled to recover Helen's supremacy by whatever means necessary.

The theme which persists in much of Grahn's work—the West's forgetfulness of its past—runs throughout the play. Among the few male figures in *The Queen of Swords* is Enki, whom Grahn notes is the "god of the wisdom of nature" (QS, 9). In a revealing metaphor, he likens modern consciousness to that first device of electronic mass media technology, the radio: "I have watched human beings/thinking they think./Really, they hear./Tuned in to radio bands/of collective understandings" (QS, 73). The metaphor of human thinking as a radio suggests that the passivity inherent in popular entertainment has the potential to make us forget, or perhaps further exacerbate the forgetting we have already done, and we must work hard to remember. Remembering entails considering how one might recall that distant time in which the influence of women was usurped by the machinations of men. The fact that this cultural moment of female dominance has been forgotten is certainly one of the negative effects of the modern age. Recognition of the shortcomings of contemporary culture helps the play qualify its embrace of the popular. The "collective understandings" Enki mentions evoke the Jungian "collective unconscious" that makes other appearances in *The Queen of Swords*.[42] These "collective understandings" suggest a uniformity of thought in humanity that seems to explain for Grahn the persistence of the Helen figure—even if she has lost much of her social standing over time.

The play's version of a Greek chorus, its crows,[43] represent a certain postmodern abandon to the pleasures of subversive wordplay. Grahn's crows possess a fluidity of identity which is apparent in her description of them in the list of dramatis personae: "*Seven*

Crows, *variously crows, dikes, Amazon warriors, motorcyclists, judges, demons*" (QS, 9. Grahn's emphasis). Like their constantly fluctuating identity, the speech of the crows is marked by a number of linguistic and semantic slippages which suggest an instability of the signifying system. The very denotative capacity of language itself is thus questioned, especially in Scene Two where the confidence Helen is gaining in her memory causes her to grow more aggressive, both verbally and physically. Her new physicality is manifested when she begins brandishing a sword. The crows offer an amusing commentary to complement the action, calling Helen by one of her other names, "Venus":

> *Crow*
> What is Venus doing I wonder?
> *Crow*
> She's doing some swordplay.
> *Crow*
> She's handling a big pricking stick.
> *Crow*
> That's cutting.
> *Crow*
> It's CAWstick.
> *Crow*
> She's practicing being a matador.
> *Crow*
> She's spearing Taurus.
> Crow
> She's trying to cut through all that bull. (QS, 80–81)

The term "swordplay," minus its initial letter "s," is of course "wordplay" and as Helen practices her sword work the crows practice their word acrobatics. Here the proverbial sense of "cutting through the bull," or getting to the heart of a matter, acquires an ironic sense in light of the fact that Helen's husband is Dumuzi, the bull god. One way of reading this passage is to conclude Helen is mimicking slaying him with his own phallus ("big pricking

Chapter Five

stick") and this passage recalls the phallic imagery present in the "wands" of Grahn's earlier long poem. Clearly this appropriation of the sword is an act of empowerment, but it is rendered in a context of puns which evoke a distinctively postmodern playfulness. One finds exchanges such as this in other long poems from the period such as in the texts of Merrill, Dorn, or Koch. The dialogue of the crows in this scene furthers the playful elements of the text we saw earlier, for instance, in Ereshkigal's characterization of herself. There is little doubt that Grahn believes in the importance of her message, but she uses the crows to qualify the imagery and symbolism of the play so that Helen's handling of a "big stick," for instance, does not trouble the reader (or viewer) as naively Freudian. Self-consciously tongue-in-cheek moves such as this go quite a distance toward making Grahn's pursuit of an alternative origin appear more fair-minded and well-considered because she takes pains to indicate to us that she is aware of the overtones and implications of her work.

Slightly later in the text, the crows call attention to the "low" nature of their humor by commenting on their consistent use of puns:

> *Crow*
> I *hate* puns—
> *Crow*
> How ungrateful—
> *Crow*
> The Gateful Dread—
> *Crow*
> A pun is the lowest form of twit—
> *Crow*
> All life is hereby condamned to death—
> *Crow*
> Condomed to which?
> *Crow*
> A condomnation of death to life— (QS, 96. Grahn's emphasis)

This dialogue, which is only a short excerpt of pages of puns that appear in the play, comes in the middle of Helen's transformation in a section called "Judgment of Helen"—itself a pun on the phrase the "Judgment of Heaven" (as well as an inversion of the "Judgment of Paris," the ultimate cause of the Trojan War). Here Helen is trying to recover her memory through much struggling, although the process appears to be working as Ereskigal tells her "[Y]ou're on your way to being a goddess,/of sagacity, at least" (*QS*, 97). This important change in Helen's person is contrasted with the inane chatter of the crows which consists of an allusion to a popular rock band, The Grateful Dead, whose name is transmuted into a pun on the various "gates" Helen must pass through in her metamorphosis. This is in addition to wordplay ("condamned to death") that adds very little to our understanding of Helen's situation. The flippant humor of the crows, then, is starkly contrastive with the life-altering process Helen goes through in increasing her power. Ultimately, the crows help Grahn qualify her work by adding a dimension of self-awareness that acknowledges the potential skepticism of the reader or viewer. She signals to us, through the crows' subversive wordplay, that she recognizes the leap of faith she asks of us in regarding Helen's attempt to overcome centuries of gender inequity through the simple process of remembering her past.

The images of popular culture—the B movie, the radio, the rock band—that persist in *The Queen of Swords* help to validate Grahn's originary approach. Were she to produce "neomyths" without trying to show how they correspond to the current era, if they were placed in some imagined mythic past as H. D. does in *Helen in Egypt*, it would be more difficult to grasp the relevance of her argument. An awareness of the historical significance of cosmetics in *The Queen of Wands*, for instance, helps tie "Helen in Hollywood" to ancient women-centered rites. On the other end of the spectrum, tonally, the playful aspects of *The Queen of Swords* further the "contemporaneity" of myth by imposing a late twentieth-century sense of humor that works to qualify the mythmak-

Chapter Five

ing process. In both cases, the return of the goddess is ultimately shown to be a process of remembering in our time and it is within the power of women to help each other remember, as *The Queen of Swords* takes pains to dramatize. This remembering is to be embellished with a recognition of the alternative lifestyles available to women now that further their independence from men.

A Chronicle of Queens is thus a fusion of disparate sources and impulses: ancient myth, Hollywood, lesbian revisionism, rock bands, and the tradition of the long poem, not to mention a self-conscious (re)construction of origins all meet in its pages. We can situate Grahn's project within the context of the postmodern long poem and its practitioners who integrate popular culture into the matrix of the poem where modernism sought to escape the popular and retreat into the sanctity of high culture. Grahn is one among many, then, who bridge the gap between high and low. As we saw with Derek Walcott in chapter 3, she also gives voice to the historically marginalized and through this process offers them a mythology not subject to the conditions imposed by patriarchy. She has indeed forged "a new myth of origins" for later writers to use as their own starting place and has given women a method by which they can regain, and amplify, their forgotten power.

Endnotes

1. Storey writes, "In the late eighteenth, throughout the nineteenth, and into the early part of the twentieth century, different groups of intellectuals . . . 'invented' the first concept of popular culture. In fact these debates eventually produced two definitions of popular culture. The first was popular culture as a quasi-mythical rural 'folk culture,' and the other—and it was very much the 'other'—was popular culture as the degraded 'mass culture' of the new urban-industrial working class" (*Inventing Popular Culture: From Folklore to Globalization* [Malden, MA: Blackwell, 2003], 1).

2. Storey, *Inventing Popular Culture*, 64. Storey cites other theorists, such as Andreas Huyssen who writes, "To a large extent, it is by the distance we have traveled from this 'great divide' between mass

culture and modernism that we can measure our own cultural postmodernity" (*After the Great Divide: Modernism, Mass Culture, Postmodernism* [Bloomington: Indiana University Press, 1986], 57). In his use of the term "mass culture" Huyssen echoes Frankfurt School theorists like Theodor W. Adorno and Max Horkheimer who form part of the critique of his book.

3   Terry Eagleton, *The Illusions of Postmodernism* (Oxford: Blackwell, 1996), viii. Eagleton, like Storey, relates the advent of postmodernism to historical circumstances and finds in it a combination of high and low culture that is the product of our economic system: "[Postmodernism] springs from an historic shift in the West to a new form of capitalism—to the ephemeral, decentralized world of technology, consumerism and the culture industry, in which service, finance and information industries triumph over traditional manufacture, and classical class politics yield ground to a diffuse range of 'identity politics.' Postmodernism is a style of culture which reflects something of this epochal change, in a depthless, decentered, ungrounded, self-reflexive, playful, derivative, eclectic, pluralistic art which blurs the boundaries between 'high' and 'popular' culture, as well as art and everyday experience" (vii).

4   Ezra Pound, *Guide to Kulchur* (London: Peter Owen, 1966), 194.

5   See note 2 above.

6   Dorn says, "I consider one thing as good as another, whether it arises from science or the so-called humanities, the newspaper or a bubblegum wrapper. All that's equal to me, as source" (Quoted in Christopher Beach, "Migrating Voices in the Poetry of Edward Dorn," *Contemporary Literature* 32 [Summer 1991]: 223).

7   As David Lehman points out, the sources of these poems are popular children's literature; in the case of "Europe" it is an "Edwardian book for girls" called *Beryl of the Bi-plane* and in "The Skaters" the inspiration comes from a book called *Three Hundred Things a Bright Boy Can Do* published in 1911 (*The Last Avant-Garde: The Making of the New York School of Poets* [New York: Anchor Books, 1999], 121–122; 160).

8   In her collected poems from 1978, Judy Grahn writes, "I wanted, in 1969, to read something which described regular, everyday women

without making us look either superhuman or pathetic" (*The Work of a Common Woman: The Collected Poetry of Judy Grahn, 1964–1977* [New York: St. Martin's Press, 1978], 60). In her introduction to the book, Adrienne Rich remarks, "The 'common woman' is in fact the embodiment of the extraordinary will-to-survive in millions of women, a life-force that transcends childbearing: an unquenchable chromosomatic reality" (18). See also Johanna Dehler's book for a discussion of Grahn and the notion of the "common" woman (*Fragments of Desire: Sapphic Fictions in Works by H. D., Judy Grahn, and Monique Wittig* [New York: Peter Lang, 1999], 71–90).

9 Judy Grahn, *The Queen of Wands* (Trumansburg, NY: The Crossing Press, 1982), xi. Hereafter cited in the text as QW.

10 Judy Grahn, *The Queen of Swords* (Boston: Beacon Press, 1987), x. Hereafter cited in the text as QS.

11 Critical attention of Grahn's examination of sexuality includes Sylvia B. Henneberg's study of *The Queen of Wands*. She notes that the figure of Helen at one point in the poem "assumes a lesbian identity which, once recognized by the reader, can be traced throughout . . . all of *The Queen of Wands.*" Henneberg finally decides that in *Wands* Grahn "does away with compulsory heterosexuality and maternity" ("When Helen Awakens: Revisionary Myth in Judy Grahn's *The Queen of Wands,*" *Women's Studies* 29.3 [June 2000]. Ebscohost. 3 March 2006. <http://web.ebscohost.com>).

12 Helen Sword, "James Merrill, Sylvia Plath, and the Poetics of Ouija," *American Literature* 66 (September 1994): 556.

13 T. S. Eliot, *Selected Prose*, ed. Frank Kermode (New York: Harvest, 1975), 177–78.

14 We should recall the argument of John B. Vickery reviewed in the introduction that modernism tends to speak "elegiacally," out of a sense of loss for that which has been left behind in the past ("Frazer and the Elegiac: The Modernist Connection," in *Modernist Anthropology: From Fieldwork to Text*, ed. Marc Manganaro [Princeton: Princeton University Press, 1990], 51).

15 Marc Manganaro asserts that the use of myth in modernism descends from James Frazer's *The Golden Bough* (1890) and allows

figures like Eliot to assume a "voice of authority." On Eliot's notion of the mythical method, Manganaro writes, "The method, in the end, pays tribute to the genius of the arranger: 'making the modern world possible for art' becomes, in practice, the artist making the modern world in his own image" (*Myth, Rhetoric, and the Voice of Authority: A Critique of Frazer, Eliot, Frye, and Campbell* [New Haven: Yale University Press, 1992], 79).

16 Judy Grahn, *Blood, Bread, and Roses: How Menstruation Created the World* (Boston: Beacon Press, 1993), 7.

17 Sue-Ellen Case, "Judy Grahn's Gynopoetics: *The Queen of Swords,*" *Studies in the Literary Imagination* 21.2 (Fall 1988): 51.

18 Case, "Judy Grahn's Gynopetics," 51.

19 Case, "Judy Grahn's Gynopetics," 51. Johanna Dehler has examined the influence Sappho has exerted on Grahn's "mythmaking" and concludes that "both Sappho and Grahn construct a different philosophical paradigm based upon a new definition of desire, identity, beauty, and cultural origin" ("Lesbos Revisited: Judy Grahn's *The Queen of Swords* as Sapphic Mythmaking," in *Women, Creators of Culture*, ed. Ekaterini Georgoudaki [Thessaloniki, Greece: Hellenic Association of American Studies, 1997], 205–206).

20 See especially Hutton's discussion in chapter 2 of his book where he provides an historical overview of the attempts to "find" a Goddess and also pages 278–282 which detail later developments (*The Triumph of the Moon: A History of Modern Pagan Witchcraft* [New York: Oxford University Press, 1999]).

21 One thinks of other occult-based texts in postmodernism. I have already noted the use of the Ouija Board in James Merrill and Sylvia Plath. The Tarot figures in Thomas Pynchon's *Gravity's Rainbow* (1973) and Italo Calvino's *The Castle of Crossed Destinies* (1977). In Grahn's use of the Tarot there has been a movement beyond the forbidding vision of "Madame Sosostris" and her "wicked pack of cards" present in Eliot's *The Waste Land* (1922) (*The Waste Land: A Facsimile and Transcript of The Original Drafts Including the Annotations of Ezra Pound*, ed. Valerie Eliot [New York: Harvest, 1971], 136). Instead the Tarot recognizes the female element in Grahn's cultural

Chapter Five

heritage and by using it as an overarching metaphor she is able to "divine" a more hopeful future. We will see magical imagery persist in *The Queen of Wands*.

22 She mentions Graves' work in her foreword to Betty De Shong Meador's translation from Enheduanna (*Inanna, Lady of the Largest Heart: Poems of the Sumerian High Priestess Enheduanna* [Austin: University of Texas Press, 2000], xiv) and in her own book *Blood, Bread and Roses* (xxii).

23 Graves' lover and fellow poet Laura Riding is often viewed as the model for the White Goddess, an idea she resented. See Deborah Baker, *In Extremis: The Life of Laura Riding* (New York: Grove Press, 1993), 401–403.

24 Robert Graves, *The White Goddess: A Historical Grammar of Poetic Myth* (New York: Noonday, 1966), 9–10.

25 Graves, *White Goddess*, 17.

26 Judy Grahn, Forward to Betty De Shong Meador, *Inanna, Lady of the Largest Heart*, xii.

27 Popular literature from the period attests to the persistence of the Goddess through a constantly shifting collection of names. Merlin Stone, for instance, in 1976 writes, "[I]t becomes clear that so many of the names used in diverse areas were simply various titles of the Great Goddess . . . We are not, however, confronting a confusing myriad of deities, but a variety of titles resulting from diverse languages and dialects, yet each referring to a most similar female divinity. Once gaining this broader and more overall view, it becomes evident that the female deity in the Near and Middle East was revered as Goddess—much as people today think of God" (*When God Was a Woman* [New York: Harvest, 1976], 22). The list of Helen's names in Grahn has been shown to be a strategy also of H. D. in her long poems. See Jan Montefiore, "'What Words Say': Three Women Poets Reading H. D.," *Agenda* 25.3–4 (Autumn/Winter 1988): 186.

28 The relationship between Grahn and H. D. has been examined by a number of critics. Jan Montefiore writes about H. D.'s relationship to later women writers. She concludes, "In Judy Grahn's evocation of female 'godhead' represented by the divine weaver Helen, her reading

and memories of H. D.'s poetry clearly help her, like [Adrienne] Rich and [Denise] Levertov, to find the numinous in the actual—but in a less sophisticated way" ("'What Words Say': Three Women Poets Reading H. D.," 186). Lynn Keller has examined the relationship of Grahn to H. D. and another important figure, Gertrude Stein, in lesbian poetics. Keller writes: "I propose that in her bringing together of precedent strategies of Stein and H. D., Grahn approaches these forebears as a butch/femme couple" (*Forms of Expansion: Recent Long Poems by Women* [Chicago: University of Chicago Press, 1997], 67). She concludes that "[T]he process undergone by Grahn's Helen is, in part, a movement from the archetypal femininity of H. D.'s Helen to a fem identity freed from the hobbles of patriarchally determined femininity" (68). In Keller's view, Grahn's Helen is finally successful in overcoming the obscurity forced on her by male authorities.

29 The influence of Betty De Shong Meador, Jungian analyst and translator of Sumerian texts is acknowledged in Grahn's Foreword to Meador's book, *Inanna, Lady of the Largest Heart*. In her work on poetics, *The Highest Apple*, Grahn calls for an "art based on our collective consciousness and collective unconsciousness" (*The Highest Apple: Sappho and the Lesbian Poetic Tradition* [San Francisco: Spinsters Ink, 1985], 87). Jung's influence on *The Queen of Swords* will also be evident later in this chapter.

30 Her speech is often filled with doubts and hesitations: "*Helen says, 'I am awake, no trance, though I move as one in a dream.'* But again she reassures herself. She had said of herself and Achilles in Egypt, *'we were not, we are not shadows'* and she had insisted that *'the hosts surging beneath the Walls, (no more than I) are ghosts'*" (H. D., *Helen in Egypt* [New York: New Directions, 1961], 43. H. D.'s emphasis).

31 Grahn notes, "the Greek word cosmetikos [carries the] dual meaning of a 'sense of harmony and order' and 'one skilled in adorning,' from cosmos, meaning both 'ornament' and 'the universe as a well-ordered whole.' Expanding on this, I use cosmetic metaform to mean the ordering of the world through descriptive use of the human body action, artful movement, shape, ornament, and decoration" (*Blood, Bread, and Roses*, 22–23). Angus Fletcher similarly notes how

Chapter Five

"kosmos" includes notions of "ornament" and to "adorn" in *Allegory: The Theory of a Symbolic Mode* (Ithaca: Cornell University Press, 1964), 117–18.

32 Grahn, *Blood, Bread, and Roses,* 75; 77.

33 Grahn, *Blood, Bread, and Roses,* 7.

34 In another poem, Grahn writes, "I have come to claim/Marilyn Monroe's body/for the sake of my own" (Grahn, *Work of a Common Woman,* 31). The speaker promises to "take [Monroe] in this paper sack/around the world, and/write on it:—the poems of Marilyn Monroe—" (32). The poem, like "Helen in Hollywood," is an attempt to recover the archetypal American woman and concludes with an image of the poem's speaker striking men with Monroe's bones.

35 This might also be an ironic allusion to Edgar Allan Poe's "Annabel Lee," a poem that records the doomed relationship of its speaker and his lover. We might also recall Poe's "To Helen" which speaks of the "glory that was Greece/And the grandeur that Rome." It is clearly against this classicism that Grahn's project works.

36 Texts in this vein include those by Dorn, Koch, Merrill and the others cited earlier. Paul Muldoon's *Madoc: A Mystery* (1991) might be another example of this kind of long poem. In *Madoc* the aspiration of Samuel Taylor Coleridge and Robert Southey to found a utopian community in northern Pennsylvania is circumvented by a science fiction–style alien attack. Perhaps even more relevant to Grahn's interests is the other long poem from the period to use Sumerian sources: *The Tablets* by Armand Schwerner, the subject of my chapter 2. Schwerner's poem uses linguistic and textual play to question the modern perspective we inevitability bring to any historical document. Like Schwerner, Grahn will foreground wordplay in *The Queen of Swords*.

37 We should recall how sexuality in Charles Olson's Hittite translation reviewed in chapter 2 is similarly less inhibited, although Olson would certainly appear a patriarchal figure to Grahn.

38 A translation of this tale by Betty De Shong Meador is appended to the play.

39 Johanna Dehler, "Lesbos Revisited," 213.

40 See note 6 above.

41 To Grahn's mind, Ereshkigal is an archetypal figure who like Helen persists over the ages: "In later stories Ereshkigal was vilified, and her human counterparts were burned at the stake, tortured, and driven underground; she remained in variants of the Inanna stories as 'the wicked queen,' the 'dark Morgan, Queen of Fairy' (Morgan Le Fay), 'the evil stepmother,' and so on" (*QS*, 164).

42 Elsewhere Ereshkigal speaks of the "four kinds of memory" Helen must work on recovering, the third of which she tells Helen is "the collective, consciously connected/recollections of your kind" (*QS*, 97; 98). This emphasis on the "conscious" nature of the "collective" imagination appears a revision of Jung's famous "collective unconscious." It speaks to the process of actively remembering that Helen dramatizes in the text.

43 Another long poem from the period uses crows in an examination of alternative religion and myth, namely Ted Hughes's *Crow* (1970).

Conclusion: Origins and the Modern/Postmodern Divide

The four long poems I have analyzed by Armand Schwerner, Judy Grahn, Derek Walcott, and Geoffrey Hill each examine the past's continuity with the present as it is figured through originary thinking. These writers adopt different points of view on this issue, however. For Grahn, considering one's origins entails rethinking the function of myth in present-day society. Her method differs from the modernists who preceded her in her embrace of popular culture—a clear indicator of her postmodernity. Walcott considers how his postcolonial position mediates his relationship to Homer. Walcott uses motifs (such as the voyage as a metaphor for self-discovery) and characters (Helen, Achilles, etc.) that first appear in Homer. To qualify his borrowings, he employs a distinctive self-reflexivity. In Hill we witness a contemporary poet thinking over his relation to history and ultimately rejecting views of Britain's Anglo-Saxon period as the definitive origin of the modern British nation. This is a process which questions the very relevance of originary thinking. Schwerner goes further than these other writers by outright parodying the search for origins that persists throughout modernist works.

Each of these writers utilizes some device common to postmodern literature: popular culture and play in Grahn, self-reflexivity in Walcott, anachronism in Hill, parody in Schwerner. Each focuses

Conclusion: Origins and the Modern/Postmodern Divide

his or her examination of origins through solitary figures: Grahn with a composite Helen, Walcott through a transformed Homer as Omeros, Hill in the form of the Anglo-Saxon King Offa, and Schwerner through his fictive "scholar/translator." This strategy is reminiscent of the epic's focus on a single figure, even if there is the twist here that Helen, Omeros, the scholar/translator, and Offa are not the heroic characters we find in the classical epic such as Odysseus or Achilles. Grahn, Schwerner, Walcott, and Hill each reevaluate themes and concerns central to writers from the first half of the century. Grahn appropriates and transmutes the myth-obsession of modernism. Walcott filters the epic tradition revived by figures such as Pound and Olson through his Caribbean consciousness. Schwerner uses the scholarly conventions of translation to critique the desire for a connection with the past. Hill responds to modernist enthusiasm for Anglo-Saxonism. All of this is to say that family resemblances persist among these otherwise strikingly disparate poets.

Although *Mercian Hymns* (1971), *The Queen of Wands* (1982), *Omeros* (1990), and *The Tablets* (1999) cover the last three decades of the twentieth century and thus sit comfortably not only within the conceptual but also within the historical framework of postmodernism, I should nevertheless also emphasize the differences in their poets' perspectives. These writers were selected for their differing national origins (Grahn and Schwerner as Americans, Walcott from St. Lucia, Hill a native-born Englishman), and their differences in race (Walcott with a "mixed" ancestry) and sexual orientation (Grahn as a lesbian). Of course these four writers do not represent all of the identities or political positions currently available in postmodernism, but they at least gesture to the breadth of diversity which postmodernity embraces in its insistence on plurality. They also hint at the host of writers who have used the long poem as a tool for an inquiry into the past in the latter half of the twentieth century. Postmodern long poems often posit alternative histories neglected by the white, male-centered poetics of mainstream modernism, as we found in Grahn's and Walcott's revisionary poems.

Chapter Six

Grahn, Schwerner, Walcott, and Hill contrast in their approaches to originary thinking as well. Because of her desire to promote a view of culture (and literature) based around women, Grahn feels she must fabricate the origin herself; she thus rejects the historical and patriarchal view of the source of Western culture and literature in Homeric Greece. Walcott is more ambivalent about Homer as a literary origin. He grapples with the ancient poet's influence on postcolonial culture throughout *Omeros*. He ultimately shows Homer can be made relevant only by being rendered in the image of a native islander and thereby incorporated into St. Lucia's way of life. Schwerner, as has been shown, sympathizes with desires to seek origins, but ultimately remains dubious of them. Geoffrey Hill decides it is his duty to question originary thinking by pointing out the historical dislocations that result from trying to peer into the past to identify the source of the present. King Offa finally appears ridiculous in *Mercian Hymns* because his point of view belongs to another age.

These poets thus differ in their evaluation of the function of originary thinking in present-day society. Hill and Schwerner abandon the search for origins altogether. Grahn, on the other hand, finds use for it, albeit in a form modified from what she finds among the male modernists who came before her. Walcott, perhaps, falls somewhere in between Grahn's reworking of originary thinking and Hill's repudiation of it. Walcott illustrates how Achille's search for his African roots in *Omeros* fails to make good on the promise of individuation, even though Achille's journey represents a movement beyond the slavish obedience the colonizer's god seeks to enforce in him.

Despite the fact that these writers bear out my premise that postmodernists have taken up the search for origins initiated by modernist writers and consistently altered it, they also indicate that origins are still a considerable problem in postmodernity. Recognizing this fact has consequences for the way we read modernism and postmodernism. While I would not suggest we completely jettison the categories—indeed I believe they hold heuristic value and thus I have used them here—we should recognize that there

Conclusion: Origins and the Modern/Postmodern Divide

is a greater fluidity between the periods than is typically admitted. The persistence of origins in twentieth-century poetry suggests there is a difference of degree, not kind, in the literary movements that literary historians divide from one another by World War II. Given our own position at the outset of the twentieth-first century, we are beginning to gain the historical perspective necessary to look at the literature of the last century as a whole. As this study demonstrates, considering how writers respond to themes like origins allows us to identify the ways in which postmodernism responds to modernism.

We clearly gain a broader view of twentieth-century poetry from this process of reevaluating the assumed modernism/postmodernism divide. I want to be careful of minimizing the differences between the two periods, however. For instance, I would maintain that they are antithetical in their relations to social equality. Modernism is generally elitist in orientation. Postmodernism, on the other hand, is more inclusive by nature. Their approaches and general ethos are also contrastive. Modernism is typically difficult and serious; postmodernism is less densely allusive and more interested in play. However, if the theme of origins is any indication, they engage some of the same cultural problems. Striking a balance between promoting difference and recognizing similarity in modernism and postmodernism is no doubt a difficult endeavor. Yet for all its challenges this is a balance we should strive to maintain in our critical views so that we can recognize the dialectic of continuity and change that marks the twentieth century's literary practices.

We have seen that studying origins in the long poem opens up other topics, such as our understanding of manifestations of the nation as they appear in twentieth-century poetry. Chapter 4 focused exclusively on Geoffrey Hill's struggle with the nationalist impulses that become apparent when the origin of Britain is identified as Anglo-Saxon. Derek Walcott's work also engages issues of national identity. As a native of St. Lucia, Walcott speaks from a site of past European imperial activities, and he thus represents a figure outside of the American and British literary traditions that typically are considered in studies of the long poem. Walcott seeks to represent the aftereffects of empire by using characters of his own invention as well as those he inherits from the classical epic. The goodwill expressed between his characters at his poem's end suggests that the island will be unified in a manner that gestures toward nationhood. However, this is not a nation with the imperialistic motivations common to those foreign powers that long sought to occupy St. Lucia—namely, England and France. In contrast to Walcott's marginal status, Geoffrey Hill speaks from a position resolutely at the center of the old English empire. As we have seen, however, Hill acknowledges the historical grievances which are leveled at his homeland. He is just as critical of England's past as Walcott is, registering his contempt for British imperialistic endeavors in India in "An Apology for the Revival of Christian Architecture in England."

Judy Grahn, however, does not focus on the nation. For Grahn, gender issues supercede concerns with nationalism. In fact her poem is resolute in overlooking local differences like national boundaries in its mission to depict the subjugation of women that has marked Western culture for millennia. Her Helen is a combination of a number of mythological figures culled from different story-telling traditions and is informed by contemporary feminism. Grahn is thus concerned with the global where Walcott is focused on St. Lucia as a microcosm for postcolonial struggle. Walcott is similar to Grahn, however, in that he offers women a prominent place in his poem through his use of figures such as Helen and Maud. By comparison, women occupy relatively little space in Hill's *Mercian Hymns*,[1] although we might recall the imagery from Hill's other poem we reviewed in chapter 4, "An Apology for the Revival of Christian Architecture in England," in which "In grange and cottage girls rise from their beds // by candlelight and mend their ruined braids." This image suggests a renewal of English culture after many centuries of decay, with women taking an important role in this change. Nevertheless, these are hardly individuated women in the sense that Grahn's Helen is at the close of *The Queen of Swords* and that Walcott's Helen is at least on her way

Conclusion: Origins and the Modern/Postmodern Divide

to becoming, if she has not become so already, at *Omeros's* end.

Schwerner's concerns are more formal as he re-envisions a modernist sensibility in a text always on the verge of falling apart. Like Pound's narrator who lamented at the end of *The Cantos* that he could not "make it cohere," Schwerner's scholar/translator is left with uncertainty as the only product of his research seems to be uncovering of an image of himself in the past.[2] In this way Schwerner critiques figures, like Charles Olson's in *The Maximus Poems*, who insist on their ability to shape perceptions of the past by engaging in origin seeking.

Thinking about origins thus allows us to consider a number of side issues, such as nationalism and gender equality, in a context which also permits us to look at the poetic output of the last century as a whole. We have seen how poets with styles and social agenda as diverse as T. S. Eliot, Ezra Pound, H. D., Basil Bunting, Louise Glück, Christopher Logue, and Seamus Heaney all engage in a search for, or examination of, origins. Originary thinking clearly holds a pervasive influence over twentieth-century poetry. Whether or not origins will factor into the next age's response to twentieth-century poetics' obsession with the present's continuity with the past will remain to be seen. It is possible that the search for origins will end with the century that devoted so much time and effort to its consideration. Such a possibility seems unlikely, however, since origin seeking appears fundamental to the human desire to know and understand the past. The fact that this desire has been scrutinized by postmodernists such as Schwerner and Hill, as I have said, should be regarded as proof of its persistence as a concern for poets rather than evidence that interest in origins is waning. Even if poets are deeply questioning origins, they are still talking about them. We will see if this dialogue persists into the next generation of poets.

Endnotes

1   The only mentions of women come in hymn XXI which notes "The young women wept and surrendered" as Offa's "province" is

Chapter Six

"fanfared" by "Cohorts of charabancs" and the "Troll-wives, groaners in sweetness, tooth-bewitchers" of hymn XXVI (Geoffrey Hill, *New and Collected Poems: 1952–1992* [New York: Houghton Mifflin, 1994], 113). The world of *Mercian Hymns* is clearly a man's world in which women appear only en masse.

2   Ezra Pound, *The Cantos* (New York: New Directions, 1995), 816.

Bibliography

Altieri, Charles. "Motives in Metaphor: John Ashbery and the Modernist Long Poem." *Genre* 11.4 (Winter 1978): 653–87.

Anderson, Benedict. *Imagined Communities: Reflections on the Origin and Spread of Nationalism.* Revised Ed. New York: Verso, 1991.

Appiah, Kwame Anthony. "The Postcolonial and the Postmodern." Ashcroft et al 119–124.

Ashcroft, Bill, Gareth Griffiths, and Helen Tiffin, eds. *The Post-Colonial Studies Reader.* New York: Routledge, 1995.

Baker, Deborah. *In Extremis: The Life of Laura Riding.* New York: Grove Press, 1993.

Baker, Peter. *Obdurate Brilliance: Exteriority and the Modern Long Poem.* Gainesville: University of Florida Press, 1991.

Bakhtin, Mikhail. *Problems of Dostoevsky's Poetics.* Trans. Caryl Emerson. Minneapolis: University of Minnesota Press, 1984.

—. *Rabelais and His World.* Trans. Helene Iswolsky. Bloomington: Indiana University Press, 1984.

Beach, Christopher. "Migrating Voices in the Poetry of Edward Dorn." *Contemporary Literature* 32 (Summer 1991): 211–228.

Bernstein, Michael André. *The Tale of the Tribe: Ezra Pound and the Modern Verse Epic.* Princeton: Princeton University Press, 1980.

Berryman, John. *The Dream Songs.* New York: Noonday, 1996.

Best, Steven and Douglas Kellner. *Postmodern Theory: Critical Interrogations.* New York: Guilford Press, 1991.

Bhabha, Homi K. *The Location of Culture.* New York: Routledge, 1994.

—, ed. *Nation and Narration*. New York: Routledge, 1990.
Bloom, Harold. Introduction. *Somewhere is Such a Kingdom: Poems 1952–1971*. By Geoffrey Hill. Boston: Houghton Mifflin, 1975. xiii–xxv.
Bolton, Jonathan. "Empire and Atonement: Geoffrey Hill's 'An Apology for the Revival of Christian Architecture in England.'" *Contemporary Literature* 38.2 (Summer 1997). Ebscohost. 9 Feb. 2006 <http://web.ebscohost.com>.
Bradshaw, David, ed. *A Concise Companion to Modernism*. Malden, MA: Blackwell, 2003.
Bunting, Basil. *The Complete Poems*. Ed. Richard Caddel. New York: Oxford University Press, 1994.
Burnett, Paula. *Derek Walcott: Politics and Poetics*. Gainesville: University of Florida Press, 2000.
Butler, Judith. "Imitation and Gender Subordination." *Literary Theory: An Anthology*. Eds. Julie Rivkin and Michael Ryan. Malden, MA.: Blackwell, 1998. 722–730.
Butterick, George F. *A Guide to "The Maximus Poems" of Charles Olson*. Berkeley: University of California Press, 1980.
Byrd, Don. *Charles Olson's "Maximus."* Urbana: University of Illinois Press, 1980.
Caddel, Richard and Peter Quartermain, eds. *Other: British and Irish Poetry Since 1970*. Hanover: Wesleyan University Press, 1999.
Case, Sue-Ellen. "Judy Grahn's Gynopoetics: *The Queen of Swords*." *Studies in the Literary Imagination* 21.2 (Fall 1988): 47–67.
Clark, Tom. *Charles Olson: The Allegory of a Poet's Life*. New York: W.W. Norton, 1991.
Conte, Joseph. *Unending Design: The Forms of Postmodern Poetry*. Ithaca: Cornell University Press, 1991.
De Man, Paul. *Blindness and Insight: Essays in the Rhetoric of Contemporary Criticism*. 2nd Ed. Minneapolis: University of Minnesota Press, 1983.
Dehler, Johanna. *Fragments of Desire: Sapphic Fictions in Works by H. D., Judy Grahn, and Monique Wittig*. New York: Peter Lang, 1999.

—. "Lesbos Revisited: Judy Grahn's *The Queen of Swords* as Sapphic Mythmaking." *Women, Creators of Culture*. Ed. Ekaterini Georgoudaki. Thessaloniki,Greece: Hellenic Association of American Studies, 1997. 205–216.
Derrida, Jacques. *A Derrida Reader*. Ed. Peggy Kamuf. New York: Columbia University Press, 1991.
Dickie, Margaret. *On the Modernist Long Poem*. Iowa City: University of Iowa Press, 1986.
Dodsworth, Martin. "*Mercian Hymns*: Offa, Charlemagne and Geoffrey Hill." *Geoffrey Hill: Essays on His Work*. Ed. Peter Robinson. Philadelphia: Open University Press, 1985. 49–61.
D[oolittle], H[ilda]. *Helen in Egypt*. New York: New Directions, 1961.
Eagleton, Terry. *The Illusions of Postmodernism*. Oxford: Blackwell, 1996.
—. *Literary Theory: An Introduction*. 2nd Ed. Minneapolis: University of Minnesota Press, 1996.
Eliot, T. S. *Selected Prose*. Ed. Frank Kermode. New York: Harvest, 1975.
—. *The Use of Poetry and the Use of Criticism: Studies in the Relation of Criticism to Poetry in England*. Cambridge: Harvard University Press, 1964.
—. *The Waste Land: A Facsimile and Transcript of The Original Drafts Including the Annotations of Ezra Pound*. Ed. Valerie Eliot. New York: Harvest, 1971.
Finkelstein, Norman. *Not One of Them in Place: Modern Poetry and Jewish American Identity*. Albany: State University of New York Press, 2001.
Fletcher, Angus. *Allegory: The Theory of a Symbolic Mode*. Ithaca: Cornell University Press, 1964.
Foster, Edward. "An Interview with Armand Schwerner." *Talisman* 19 (Winter 1998/1999): 30–44.
Frantzen, Allen J. *Desire for Origins: New Language, Old English, and Teaching the Tradition*. New Brunswick: Rutgers University Press, 1990.

Bibliography

Fredman, Stephen. *The Grounding of American Poetry: Charles Olson and the Emersonian Tradition.* Cambridge: Cambridge University Press, 1993.

Friedman, Susan Stanford. "When a 'Long' Poem is a 'Big' Poem: Self-Authorizing Strategies in Women's Twentieth-Century 'Long Poems.'" *LIT* 2 (1990): 9–25.

Gardner, Thomas. *Discovering Ourselves in Whitman: The Contemporary American Long Poem.* Urbana: University of Illinois Press, 1989.

Gellner, Ernest. "Nationalism and High Cultures." Hutchinson and Smith 63–69.

Genette, Gèrard. *Palimpsests: Literature in the Second Degree.* Trans. Channa Newman and Claude Doubinsky. Lincoln: University of Nebraska Press, 1997.

Glück, Louise. *Meadowlands.* Hopewell, NJ: Ecco, 1996.

Grahn, Judy. *Blood, Bread, and Roses: How Menstruation Created the World.* Boston: Beacon Press, 1993.

—. Foreword. *Inanna, Lady of Largest Heart: Poems of the Sumerian High Priestess, Enheduanna.* By Betty De Shong Meador. Austin: University of Texas Press, 2000. xi–xvi.

—. *The Highest Apple: Sappho and the Lesbian Poetic Tradition.* San Francisco: Spinsters Ink, 1985.

—. *The Queen of Swords.* Boston: Beacon Press, 1987.

—. *The Queen of Wands.* Trumansburg, NY: The Crossing Press, 1982.

—. *The Work of a Common Woman: The Collected Poetry of Judy Grahn, 1964–1977.* New York: St. Martin's Press, 1978.

Graves, Robert. *The White Goddess: A Historical Grammar of Poetic Myth.* New York: Noonday, 1966.

Halden-Sullivan, Judith. *The Topology of Being: The Poetics of Charles Olson.* New York: Peter Lang, 1991.

Hamner, Robert D. *Epic of the Dispossessed: Derek Walcott's "Omeros."* Columbia: University of Missouri Press, 1997.

—. "Introduction to *Critical Perspectives on Derek Walcott.*" *Three Dynamite Writers: Derek Walcott, Naguib Mahfouz, Wole Soyinka.*

Ed. Donald E. Herdeck. Colorado Springs: Three Continents Press, 1995. 3–20.

Hardwick, Lorna. "Reception as Simile: The Poetics of Reversal in Homer and Derek Walcott." *International Journal of the Classical Tradition* 3.3 (Winter 1997). Ebscohost. 3 March 2006. < http://web.ebscohost.com>.

Hart, Henry. *The Poetry of Geoffrey Hill*. Carbondale: Southern Illinois University Press, 1986.

Heaney, Seamus. *Beowulf: A New Verse Translation*. New York: W.W. Norton, 2000.

—. *Poems: 1965–1975*. New York: Noonday, 1988.

Henneberg, Sylvia B. "When Helen Awakens: Revisionary Myth in Judy Grahn's *The Queen of Wands*." *Women's Studies* 29.3 (June 2000). Ebscohost. 3 March 2006. <http://web.ebscohost.com>.

Hill, Geoffrey. *Mercian Hymns*. London: Andre Deutsch, 1971.

—. *New and Collected Poems: 1952–1992*. New York: Houghton Mifflin, 1994.

Hobsbawm, Eric and Terence Ranger, eds. *The Invention of Tradition*. New York: Cambridge University Press, 1983.

Homer. *The Iliad*. Trans. Robert Fagles. New York: Penguin, 1990.

Howe, Nicholas. "Praise and Lament: The Afterlife of Old English Poetry in Auden, Hill, and Gunn." *Words and Works: Studies in Medieval English Language and Literature in Honour of Fred C. Robinson*. Eds. Peter S. Baker and Nicholas Howe. Buffalo: University of Toronto Press, 1998. 293–310.

Hutcheon, Linda. "Circling the Downspout of Empire." Ashcroft et al. 130–135.

—. *A Poetics of Postmodernism: History, Theory, Fiction*. New York: Routledge, 1988.

Hutchinson, John and Anthony D. Smith, eds. *Nationalism*. Oxford: Oxford University Press, 1994.

Hutton, Ronald. *The Triumph of the Moon: A History of Modern Pagan Witchcraft*. New York: Oxford University Press, 1999.

Bibliography

Huyssen, Andreas. *After the Great Divide: Modernism, Mass Culture, Postmodernism*. Bloomington: Indiana University Press, 1986.

Jameson, Fredric. *Postmodernism; or, The Cultural Logic of Late Capitalism*. Durham: Duke University Press, 1991.

Jencks, Charles. *What is Post-Modernism?* London: Academy Editions, 1996.

Jones, David. *The Anathemata: Fragments of an Attempted Writing*. Boston: Faber and Faber, 1952.

Keller, Lynn. *Forms of Expansion: Recent Long Poems by Women*. Chicago: University of Chicago Press, 1997.

Kenner, Hugh. *The Pound Era*. Berkeley: University of California Press, 1973.

Knottenbelt, E.M. *Passionate Intelligence: The Poetry of Geoffrey Hill*. Atlanta: Rodopi, 1990.

Knox, Bernard. Introduction. *The Iliad*. By Homer. Trans. Robert Fagles. New York: Penguin, 1990. 3–67.

Lavazzi, Tom. "Playing it Loose with *The Tablets*." *Talisman* 19 (Winter 1998/1999): 90–94.

Lazer, Hank. "Sacred Forgery and Grounds of Poetic Archeology: Armand Schwerner's *The Tablets*." *Chicago Review* 46.1 (2000): 142–153. Ebscohost. 14 Sept. 2006. <http://web.ebscohost.com>.

Lehman, David. *The Last Avant-Garde: The Making of the New York School of Poets*. New York: Anchor Books, 1999.

Lock, Charles. "Derek Walcott's *Omeros*: Echoes from a White-Throated Vase." *Massachusetts Review* 40.1 (Spring 2000). Ebschost. 7 March 2006. <http://web.ebscohost.com>.

Logan, William. "The Fallen World of Geoffrey Hill." *New Criterion* 12.7 (March 1994). Ebscohost. 8 Feb. 2006. <http://web.ebscohost.com>.

Logue, Christopher. *War Music: An Account of Books 1–4 and 16–19 of Homer's "Iliad."* New York: Noonday, 1997.

Lyotard, Jean-François. *The Postmodern Condition: A Report on Knowledge*. Trans. Geoff Bennington and Brian Massumi. Minneapolis: University of Minnesota Press, 1979.

Maier, John. *Gilgamesh: A Reader*. Wacuonda, IL: Bolchazy-Caduci Publishers, 1997.

Manganaro, Marc. "'Beating a Drum in a Jungle': T. S. Eliot on the Artist as 'Primitive.'" *Modern Language Quarterly* 47.4 (December 1986): 393–421.

—. *Myth, Rhetoric, and the Voice of Authority: A Critique of Frazer, Eliot, Frye, and Campbell*. New Haven: Yale University Press, 1992.

McClure, Charlotte S. "'Helen of the 'West Indies': History or Poetry of a Caribbean Realm." *Studies in the Literary Imagination* 26 (Fall 1993). Ebscohost. 3 March 2006. <http://web.ebscohost.com>.

McHale, Brian. *The Obligation Toward the Difficult Whole: Postmodernist Long Poems*. Tuscaloosa: University of Alabama Press, 2004.

—. "Topology of a Phantom City: *The Tablets* as Hoax." *Talisman* 19 (Winter 1998/1999): 86–89.

Meador, Betty De Shong. *Inanna, Lady of the Largest Heart: Poems of the Sumerian High Priestess Enheduanna*. Austin: University of Texas Press, 2000.

Milne, W.S. *An Introduction to Geoffrey Hill*. London: Bellew, 1998.

"Modernism and Postmodernism." *Princeton Encyclopedia of Poetry and Poetics*. 3rd ed. 1993.

Moffett, Joe. "Anglo-Saxon and Welsh Origins in David Jones's *The Anathemata*." *North American Journal of Welsh Studies* 6.1 (Winter 2006): 1–18.

Montefiore, Jan. "'What Words Say': Three Women Poets Reading H. D." *Agenda* 25.3-4 (Autumn/Winter 1988): 172–190.

Nagy, Gregory. *Poetry as Performance: Homer and Beyond*. New York: Cambridge University Press, 1996.

Needham, John. "The Idiom of *Mercian Hymns*," in *Geoffrey Hill*, ed. Harold Bloom (New York: Chelsea House, 1986). 77–86.

Newton, Sam. *The Origins of Beowulf and the Pre-Viking Kingdom of East Anglia*. Cambridge: D.S. Brewer, 1993.

Bibliography

Olson, Charles. *The Collected Poems, Excluding the "Maximus" Poems.* Ed. George F. Butterick. Berkeley: University of California Press, 1987.
—. *Collected Prose.* Ed. Donald Allen and Benjamin Friedlander. Berkeley: University of California Press, 1997.
—. *The Maximus Poems.* Ed. George F. Butterick. Berkeley: University of California Press, 1983.
—. *Selected Writings.* Ed. Robert Creeley. New York: New Directions, 1966.
—. *The Special View of History.* Ed. Ann Charters. Berkeley: Oyez, 1970.
Paul, Sherman. *Olson's Push: Origin, Black Mountain, and Recent American Poetry.* Baton Rouge: Louisiana State University Press, 1978.
Paz, Octavio. *The Other Voice: Essays on Modern Poetry.* New York: Harcourt Brace Jovanovich, 1991.
Pearce, Roy Harvey. *The Continuity of American Poetry.* Princeton: Princeton University Press, 1961.
Perkins, David. *A History of Modern Poetry: Modernism and After.* Cambridge: Belknap Press, 1987.
Perloff, Marjorie. *The Dance of the Intellect: Studies in the Poetry of the Pound Tradition.* New York: Cambridge University Press, 1985.
Pound, Ezra. *The Cantos.* New York: New Directions, 1995.
—. *Guide to Kulchur.* London: Peter Owen, 1966.
—. *Literary Essays.* Ed. T. S. Eliot. New York: New Directions, 1968.
—. *Personae: The Shorter Poems.* Eds. Lea Beachler and A. Walton Litz. New York: New Directions, 1990.
Ramazani, Jahan. *The Hybrid Muse: Postcolonial Poetry in English.* Chicago: University of Chicago Press, 2001.
Rich, Adrienne. Introduction. *The Work of a Common Woman.* By Judy Grahn. 7–21.
Rose, Margaret. *Parody: Ancient, Modern, and Post-Modern.* Cambridge: Cambridge University Press, 1993.

Rosenthal, M.L. and Sally Gall. *Modern Poetic Sequence: The Genius of Modern Poetry*. New York: Oxford University Press, 1986.

Rothenberg, Jerome. *Shaking the Pumpkin: Traditional Poetry of the Indian North Americas*. Garden City, NY: Doubleday, 1972.

—. *Technicians of the Sacred: A Range of Poetries from Africa, America, Asia, and Oceania*. Garden City, NY: Doubleday, 1968.

Rothenberg, Jerome and Pierre Joris. *Poems for the Millennium: Volume One*. Berkeley: University of California Press, 1995.

Ruskin, John. *Fors Clavigera: Letters to the Workmen and Labourers of Great Britain, Volume I*. Boston: Dana Estes & Company, n.d.

Said, Edward W. *Beginnings: Intention and Method*. New York: Columbia University Press, 1985.

—. *Culture and Imperialism*. New York: Vintage, 1993.

—. *Orientalism*. New York: Vintage, 1978.

Salvato, Nick. "Louis Zukofsky's Old English Sources for 'A'-23." *Notes and Queries* 49.1 (March 2002): 85–88.

Sampietro, Luigi. *Derek Walcott on "Omeros": An Interview*. 20 Sept. 2006. <http://users.unimi.it/caribana/OnOmeros.html>.

Schwerner, Armand. *Seaweed*. Los Angeles: Black Sparrow Press, 1969.

—. *The Tablets*. Orono, ME: The National Poetry Foundation, 1999.

—. *The Tablets: I–XV*. New York: Grossman Publishers, 1971.

Scroggins, Mark. *Louis Zukofsky and the Poetry of Knowledge*. Tuscaloosa: University of Alabama Press, 1998.

Sherry, Vincent. *The Uncommon Tongue: The Poetry and Criticism of Geoffrey Hill*. Ann Arbor: University of Michigan Press, 1987.

Shetley, Vernon. *After the Death of Poetry: Poet and Audience in Contemporary America*. Durham: Duke University Press, 1993.

Smith, Ian. *M5 (Birmingham to Exeter)*. 20 Sept. 2006. <http://euclid.colorado.edu/~rmg/roads/m5.html>.

Spencer, Philip and Howard Wollman. *Nationalism: A Critical Introduction*. London: Sage Publications, 2002.

Spivak, Gayatri Chakravorty. "Can the Subaltern Speak?" Ashcroft et al 24–28.
Stenton, Frank. *Anglo-Saxon England*. 3rd Ed. New York: Oxford University Press, 2001.
Stevens, Wallace. *Collected Poetry and Prose*. Eds. Frank Kermode and Joan Richardson. New York: Library of America, 1997.
Stevenson, Randall. *Modernist Fiction: An Introduction*. Lexington: University Press of Kentucky, 1992.
Stone, Merlin. *When God Was a Woman*. New York: Harvest, 1976.
Storey, John. *Inventing Popular Culture: From Folklore to Globalization*. Malden, MA: Blackwell, 2003.
Sword, Helen. "James Merrill, Sylvia Plath, and the Poetics of Ouija." *American Literature* 66 (September 1994): 553–572.
Tassoni, John Paul. "Play and Co-Option in Kenneth Koch's *Ko, or A Season on Earth*: 'Freedom and the Realizable World!'" *Sagetrieb* 10.1–2 (Spring–Fall 1991): 123–132.
Thieme, John. *Derek Walcott*. New York: Manchester University Press, 1999.
Torgovnick, Marianna. *Gone Primitive: Savage Intellects, Modern Lives*. Chicago: University of Chicago Press, 1991.
Tytell, John. *Ezra Pound: The Solitary Volcano*. New York: Anchor Press, 1987.
Vickery, John B. "Frazer and the Elegiac: The Modernist Connection." *Modernist Anthropology: From Fieldwork to Text*. Ed. Marc Manganaro. Princeton: Princeton University Press, 1990. 51–68.
Virgil. *The Aeneid*. Trans. Allen Mandelbaum. New York: Bantam, 1971.
Von Hallberg, Robert. *Charles Olson: The Scholar's Art*. Cambridge: Harvard University Press, 1978.
Walcott, Derek. *Collected Poems: 1948–1984*. New York: Farrar, Straus and Giroux, 1986.
—. *Omeros*. New York: Noonday, 1990.
—. *What the Twilight Says*. New York: Farrar, Straus and Giroux, 1998.

Walker, Jeffrey. *Bardic Ethos and the American Epic Poem: Whitman, Pound, Crane, Williams, Olson.* Baton Rouge: Louisiana State University Press, 1989.

Weil, Simone. *"The Iliad"; or the Poem of Force: A Critical Edition.* Trans. and Ed. James P. Holoka. New York: Peter Lang, 2003.

Wormald, Patrick. "The Age of Offa and Alcuin." *The Anglo-Saxons.* Ed. James Campbell. New York: Penguin, 1991. 101–131.

Yeats, William Butler. *The Yeats Reader: A Portable Compendium of Poetry, Drama, and Prose.* Revised Ed. Ed. Richard J. Finneran. New York: Scribner, 2002.

Zukofsky, Louis. *"A."* Baltimore: Johns Hopkins University Press, 1978.

Index

Achille (Walcott), 62, 67, 74, 76–83
Adorno, Theodor W., 147n2
Albion, 103–104, 120n41–42
Alfred, King, 121n46
alliteration, 19–20, 109
allusion, 19–20
Altieri, Charles, 24n4
anachronism, 16–17, 49, 51, 94, 99–102, 106–107, 154
Anderson, Benedict, 95–97, 115
Appiah, Kwame Anthony, 64–65
archaeology, 4, 26n10, 27n11, 35–38, 48, 128
Ariosto, 10
Aristotle, 37
Ashbery, John, 24n3; "Europe," "The Skaters," 124, 147n7
Auden, W. H., 31n57; "Archaeology," 27n11; "The Wanderer," 18

Baker, Peter, 54
Bakhtin, Mikhail, 43–45
Beowulf, 18, 21, 30n56, 91–92, 117n6
Bernstein, Charles, 90n40; "The Lives of the Toll Takers," 2
Bernstein, Michael André, 29n42
Berryman, John: *The Dream Songs*, 2, 90n40, 124
Bhabha, Homi K., 65–66, 73, 80, 96–97
Blake, William: *Visions of the Daughters of Albion*, 120n42
Bloodaxe, Eric, 20
Bloom, Harold, 87n22, 99
Boethius: *Consolation of Philosophy*, 106, 121n46
Bronk, William: "At Tikal," 27n11
Bunting, Basil, 22, 31n59, 92, 111, 114, 118n16, 160; *Briggflatts*, 2, 19–20, 92
Butler, Judith, 25n5
Byron, Lord: *Don Juan*, 120n42

Calvino, Italo: *The Castle of Crossed Destinies*, 149n21
carnival. *See* Bakhtin, Mikhail
Carson, Ciaran, 114

Index

Chanson de Roland, La, 105
Chaucer, Geoffrey, 121n46; "Complaint to His Purse," 120n42
Coleridge, Samuel Taylor, 152n36; *Anima Poetae,* 122n59
colonialism, 18, 63–65, 69, 74, 112–114, 132. See also postcolonialism
commercialism, 12, 37–39, 42, 100–101, 106, 121n47
confessional poetry, 2
Conte, Joseph, 24n4
cosmetics, 134–138, 151n31
Crane, Hart: *The Bridge,* 1
Creeley, Robert, 38, 41

Dante, 34, 84; *Divine Comedy,* 58n27, 71
de Man, Paul, 5–6
"Deor," 109
Derrida, Jacques, 25n5, 37
Dickie, Margaret, 3, 25n8
Dorn, Edward, 125, 141, 144, 147n6, 152n36; *Gunslinger,* 90n40, 124

Eagleton Terry, 27n16, 83, 86n18, 123, 147n3
Eliot, T. S., 5–8, 28n20, 33, 35, 55n5; "auditory imagination," 5–8, 127; "mythical method," 29n31, 126–127, 129, 148n15; *The Waste Land,* 5, 45–46, 59n37, 119n35, 149n21

Elizabeth I, Queen, 121n46
epic, 3, 14, 16–18, 21, 26n9, 29n42, 67, 72, 83–84, 85n6, 87n21, 89n33, 90n41, 155
Epic of Gilgamesh, The, 10–12
Eshleman, Clayton: *Placements,* 9
ethnopoetics, 40, 57n17

Frankfurt School. See Adorno, Theodor W.; Horkheimer, Max
Frantzen, Allen, 97–98
Frazer, James: *The Golden Bough,* 148n15
French Symbolists, 117n4
Freudian motifs, 143–144
Friedman, Susan Stanford, 25n8

Gardner, John: *Gilgamesh, The Sunlight Dialogues,* 10
Gardner, Thomas, 24n3, 84
Gellner, Ernest, 98
gender, issues of, 8, 14–16, 25n5, 124–125, 127–146, 155, 158–159, 159n1
Genette, Gérard, 49–50
Geoffrey of Monmouth: *The History of the Kings of Britain,* 26n9
Glück, Louise, 159; *Meadowlands,* 2, 15–16
goddess worship, 128–129, 141, 149n20, 150n27
Gonne, Maud, 89n29

173

Index

Grahn, Judy, 13–15, 22–23, 25n8, 116, 124–146, 147n8, 149n19, 149n21, 150n28, 151n31, 152n34–37, 153n41, 154–156, 158; *Blood, Bread, and Roses*, 127, 135, 150n22; *A Chronicle of Queens*, 124–125, 128–129, 138, 146; *The Highest Apple, Sappho and the Lesbian Poetic Tradition*, 151n29; *The Queen of Swords*, 13, 125, 127, 138–146, 151n29, 152n36, 159; *The Queen of Wands*, 2, 13, 125, 127–138, 145, 148n11, 149n21, 154–155; *The Work of a Common Woman: The Collected Poetry of Judy Grahn*, 147n8
Grateful Dead, The, 145
Graves, Robert, 149 n22; *The White Goddess*, 128–129, 139, 150n23
Gregory, Lady: *Grania*, 118n16
Gunn, Thom, 92

H. D. [Hilda Doolittle], 150n27–28, 159; *Helen in Egypt*, 2, 14–15, 130, 132–133, 145, 151n30
Heaney, Seamus, 9, 20–22, 27n11, 114, 159; "Belderg," 20–21; *Beowulf*, 18, 21, 92; "Bog poems," 21; "Kinship," 2; *North*, 21
Helen (Grahn), 129–139, 156, 158. See also Inanna / Helen
Helen (H. D.), 14–15, 132–134
Helen (Walcott), 74–76, 80–81, 87n21, 159

Henry VIII, 115
Hill, Geoffrey, 21–23, 85, 117n4, 118n26, 119n27, 119n35, 121n47, 122n59, 154–156, 158–159; "An Apology for the Revival of Christian Architecture in England," 22, 93, 112–116, 158; *For the Unfallen*, 122n60; *Mercian Hymns*, 2, 22, 55n1, 92–113, 115, 117n4, 133, 154–156, 158, 159n1; *The Orchards of Syon*, 116; *Speech! Speech!*, 116, 122n60; *Tenebrae*, 112
history, problems of understanding, 13, 34–36, 43, 82, 92, 103, 124, 142
Hobsbawm, Eric, 98
Homer, 14–18, 23, 29n32, 62–79, 82–84, 85n6, 87n21, 88n23, 89n31, 89n33, 132, 139, 154–156
Horkheimer Max, 147n2
Howe, Susan, 90n40; *The Europe of Trusts*, 2
Hughes, Ted: *Crow*, 10, 153n43
Hutcheon, Linda, 64, 66, 73, 90n40
Hutton, Ronald, 128, 149n20
Huyssen, Andreas, 124, 146n2

Iliad, 9, 14, 16–18, 63, 69, 74, 76, 83
Imagism, 14
Inanna / Helen (Grahn), 139–146, 153n41

174

Industrial Revolution, 107
Irish National Theatre, 118n16

Jameson, Fredric, 57n19, 86n18
Jencks, Charles, 40
Jones, David, 9, 20, 21, 26n9, 114; *The Anathemata*, 7, 19, 92
Joris, Pierre, 7
Joyce, James: *Ulysses*, 126
Jung, Carl, 58n20, 130; Jungian motifs, 40, 142, 151n29, 153n42

Keats, John: "On Sitting Down to Read King Lear Once Again," 120n42
Keller, Lynn, 14, 25n8, 150n28
Kenner, Hugh, 30n56
Kinnell, Galway: *The Book of Nightmares*, 1, 89n30
Koch, Kenneth, 125, 144, 152n36; *Seasons on Earth*, 10, 55n1, 84, 124
Kramer, Samuel Noah, 10, 13, 34

Lacanian psychoanalysis, 59n40
language, 12, 14, 20–21, 42, 57n15, 77–78, 80–82, 89n33, 104, 106
Language Poets, 90n40
Layamon: *Brut*, 26n9
Logue, Christopher, 159; *War Music*, 16–17
long poem, 1–4, 8–10, 16, 18–19, 24n4, 25n8, 35, 54, 84–85,
90n40, 124–125, 143, 154–155, 157–158
Lowell, Robert: *History*, 89n30
Lyotard, Jean-François, 54, 55n7

M5, 99–100, 102–103
MacDiarmid, Hugh, 9
Mackey, Nathaniel: *Song of the Andoumboulou*, 9
Maximus (character), 39, 54, 58n27
McGrath, Thomas: *Letter to an Imaginary Friend*, 84
McHale, Brian, 26n10, 55n3
Merrill, James, 24n3, 126, 149n21, 152n36; *The Changing of the Light at Sandover*, 55n1, 90n40, 125
Merwin, W. S.: *Sir Gawain and the Green Knight*, 92
metanarrative, 36, 54, 55n7
Middle English, 26n9, 92
Milton, John: *Paradise Lost*, 26n9
modernism, 1, 3–6, 8–10, 14, 22–24, 26n9, 27n14, 29n30, 31n60, 33, 35–36, 40, 43, 45–47, 55n7, 57n19, 92, 94, 111, 123–24, 126, 146, 148n15, 154–157
Monroe, Marilyn, 135–136, 138, 152n34
Morgan, Edward: *Beowulf, Dies Irae*, 92
Muldoon, Paul: *Madoc: A Mystery*, 152n36
mythology, 36, 39–42, 124–129,

Index

140, 145–146, 148n15, 153n43, 154–155

Nagy, Gregory, 85n6
naming, 29n29, 77–80, 88n25
nationalism, 8, 94–98, 118n15, 118n17, 154, 157–158
Neruda, Pablo: *Canto General*, 27n11
Nobel Prize, 17, 20, 61, 82
Norton Anthology of English Literature, The, 21

occult, 128, 149n21
Odyssey, 9, 14–16, 62
OED [Oxford English Dictionary], 2, 57n15, 99, 108, 121n47, 127
Offa, King (character), 93–96, 99–112, 114, 133, 155
Old English, 18–19, 30n57, 57n15, 92–93, 109
Olson, Charles, 10, 12–13, 20, 23–24, 28n24, 29n39, 29n42, 35–43, 46–49, 51–54, 56n7, 56n11, 57n15, 57n17, 58n20, 58n22, 58n24, 58n27, 152n37, 155; "Human Universe," 37–38, 40, 56n10; "The Kingfishers," 38, 46; *The Maximus Poems*, 12–13, 35–42, 52–54, 58n27, 159; *Mayan Letters*, 38, 41; "The Present is Prologue," 36–37; *Selected Writings*, 38, 56n10;

"Song of Ullikummi," 13, 41–42, 51–52; *The Special View of History*, 38, 56n10
oral tradition, 41
Orientalism, 6, 63–64, 97–98
origins, 1–10, 14, 25n5, 26n9, 27n11, 29n29, 36, 43, 48, 66–67, 80, 95, 97–98, 116, 127–128, 133, 154–158; African, 9, 76–81; Algonquin, 13, 39–42, 51; Anglo-Saxon, 9, 18–22, 29n32; Arthurian, 26n9; British, 118n15; Celtic, 9, 121n56; Homeric, 9, 14–18, 29n32; Paleolithic, 9; Renaissance, 9–10; Sumerian, 9–14, 29n32
Ouija Board, 125, 149n21

Paganism, 128
palimpsest, 20, 49–50
parody, 17, 19, 34, 43, 46, 51, 57n15, 154
Paz, Octavio, 1
Plath, Sylvia, 125, 149n21
play, 33, 55n1, 106, 111, 138, 143–145, 154, 157
Poe, Edgar Allan: "Annabel Lee," "To Helen," 152n35
popular culture, 12, 123–126, 134–138, 141–142, 145, 147n3, 154
postcolonialism, 8, 18, 61–66, 133, 154. *See also* colonialism
postmodernism, 1, 7–10, 22, 24,

27n16, 33, 36–37, 40, 54, 55n1,
  55n7, 57n19, 64–65, 73, 84–85,
  86n18, 90n40, 97, 123–24,
  126, 143, 146, 147n3, 154–157
poststructuralism, 25n5, 37, 96
Pound, Ezra, 4–8, 18–19, 22,
  29n42, 30n56, 33, 35, 46,
  55n5, 91–92, 94, 111, 118n16,
  124, 156; *The Cantos*, 12, 14,
  18, 30n56, 46, 53, 159; "Hugh
  Selwyn Mauberley," 4–5; "The
  Seafarer," 18, 110
primitivism, 6–8, 28n19–20,
  57n15
prose poem, 93
psychoanalysis, 47
Pynchon, Thomas: *Gravity's
  Rainbow*, 149n21

Rabelais, 43–44
Ramazani, Jahan, 88n28, 90n41
revisionism, 8, 15, 23, 62, 76, 135,
  139, 155
Rich, Adrienne, 147n8
Riding, Laura, 150n23
Riley, Peter: *Distant Points*, 9,
  27n11
Rose, Margaret, 34, 51
Rosenthal, M. L. and Sally Gall,
  24n4
Rothenberg, Jerome, 8, 40; *Poems
  for the Millennium*, 7, 28n24,
  57n15, 57n17; *Shaking the
  Pumpkin*, 8, 57n17; *Technicians
  of the Sacred*, 7–8
Route 128, 38–39
Ruskin, John: *Fors Clavigera*, 108,
  114

Said, Edward W., 6, 25n5, 63–64,
  74, 84, 97
Sandburg, Carl: *The People, Yes*, 42
Sappho, 149n19
Schliemann, Heinrich, 26n10
scholar / translator (character),
  34–35, 43–53, 59n37, 155, 159
Schwerner, Armand, 13, 19, 23–24,
  28n24, 33–36, 40, 43–54, 55n1,
  55n5, 56n7, 57n.17, 59n43, 102,
  111, 154–155, 159; *Cantos from
  Dante's Inferno*, 10; *Seaweed*, 53;
  The Tablets, 13, 33–35, 43–53,
  55n3, 59n39, 59n40, 59n43,
  60n49, 90n40, 95, 152n36,
  155–156, 160
"Seafarer, The," 18, 31n58, 91–92,
  110
self-reflexivity, 27n16, 33, 35, 48,
  52, 55n1, 62–73, 84, 86n18,
  90n40, 154
sexuality, 39–42, 51–52, 76, 135–
  139, 143–144, 152n37
Shakespeare, William: *Henry V*,
  King Lear, 120n42
signification, signifier / signified,
  42, 71–72, 79, 96–97, 101, 142
Sir Gawain and the Green Knight,
  26n9, 92, 121n56

Index

Sophocles, 34; *Philoctetes*, 69
Southey, Robert, 152n36
Spenser, Edmund: *The Fairie Queene*, 26n9, 120n42
Spivak, Gayatri, 65
Stein, Gertrude, 150n28
Stevens, Wallace, 14, 33
Stone, Merlin, 150n27
Storey, John, 123, 146n1–2, 147n3
Sutton Hoo, 26n10
Sweet's Anglo-Saxon Reader, 117n4

Tarot, 128, 149n21
Tennyson, Alfred, Lord: "The Battle of Brunanburh" 30n54; *Idylls of the King*, 26n9; *Maud: A Monodrama*, 88n29
textuality, 15, 50, 67, 70, 96, 104, 106, 111
Torgovnick, Marianna, 6

Vickery, John B., 4, 27n14, 35, 94, 111, 148n14
Virgil, 71, 121n48; *Aeneid*, 57n14, 68

Walcott, Derek, 17–18, 23, 32n73, 85n2, 87n21–23, 89n37, 154–156, 158; "The Antilles: Fragments of Epic Memory," 82; *The Joker of Seville*, 62; "The Muse of History," 85n2; *The Odyssey*, 17, 62; *Omeros*, 2, 17, 54, 62–85, 87n21, 88n25, 89n37, 90n41, 154–156, 158–159; "Origins," 67–68, 79, 88n25; "The Schooner Flight," 32n73; *Sea Grapes*, 79; *Selected Poems*, 67
Walker, Jeffrey, 24n3
"Wanderer, The," 18
Weil, Simone, 63
Whitman, Walt, 24n3, 84–85
Wicca, 128
Wilbur, Richard, 92
Williams, William Carlos, 14, 29n42, 126
wordplay, 56n11, 101, 106, 142–145, 152n36
"Wulf and Eadwacer," 109

Yeats, W. B., 20, 89n29, 126; *Cathleen ni Houlihan*, 118n16

Zukofsky, Louis, 10, 19–20, 57n19; "A," 2, 11–12, 30n57

JOE MOFFETT is Assistant Professor of English at Kentucky Wesleyan College. His essays, book reviews, and poems have appeared in such journals as *LIT: Literature Interpretation Theory*; *North American Journal of Welsh Studies*; *Rock & Sling: A Journal of Literature, Art, and Faith*; *The Journal*; and *Choice*.

www.ingramcontent.com/pod-product-compliance
Lightning Source LLC
Chambersburg PA
CBHW052046300426
44117CB00012B/2000